Adíos, Strunk & White

gary & glynis hoffman

VERVE PRESS

Adíos, Strunk & White by Gary and Glynis Hoffman
ISBN 0-937363-14-6
Library of Congress Catalog Card Number: 96-61884
Printed in the United States of America
Published by Verve Press, P.O. Box 1997, Huntington Beach, California, 92647

All rights reserved. No part of this book may be reproduced or transmitted in any form or by any means, electronic or mechanical, including photocopying, recording or by any information storage and retrieval system without written permission from the author, except for the inclusion of brief quotations in reviews and analytical essays.References to other material are used in accordance with Section 107 of the United States Copyright Act.

Copyright © 1997 by Gary and Glynis Hoffman

Printing: KNI
First Printing 1997

Cover Design: Gary Hoffman
Graphic Design: Gary Hoffman
Graphic Enhancement: Neil Hong
Page Layout: Neil Hong

Library of Congress Cataloguing-in-Publication Data
Hoffman, Gary
   Adíos, strunk & white / Gary & Glynis Hoffman
     p. cm.
   ISBN 0-937363-14-6
    1. English language — Rhetoric
    2. English language — Composition and exercises
    3. English language — Style
    4. English language — Grammar I. Hoffman,
Glynis II. Title
PE 1408 46576   96-61884
808.042   CIP

CONTENTS

ABOUT THE AUTHORS
ACKNOWLEDGEMENTS
Our Personal Netting
INTRODUCTION
The Grammar School Correction
Learning to Write Before Learning to Read
Neither a Trade Book Nor a Text Book Be
A Disclaimer

1 STYLE

Style Before Organization   12

FLOW: ways to speed pace and give smoothness   16
Freighting   17
Telescoping   22
Netting   28

PAUSE: ways to slow pace and create emphasis   36
Very Short Sentences   37
Melted-Together Words   39
Hieroglyphics   42
Super-Literalism   47

FUSION: ways to spark interest, fine-tune and
        compress   52
Recyclables   55
Break-Ups   60
Line-Ups   65
Mix Masters   68

SCRUB: ways to purge intimidation and
        anesthesia   74
Facial Packs   75
Metal Mask   78
War Paint   83

2 THOUGHT

Cracking Humpty Humpty   88

PEEL: seeking meaning	90
Inductive Analysis	91
Eclipse	95
Fallacies	99

PRESS: testing meaning	102
Deductive Thought	103
Comparison and Contrast	105
Synthesized Research	108

FILTER: expressing meaning	113
The Direct Connection	114
The Metaphor Connection	115
The Syntax Connection	116

3 FORM

Remaking Humpty Dumpty   121

TIME WARPING: ways to narrate	124
Splitting the Second	126
Flashback	132
Strip Tease	137
Raising the Dead	143

ENCIRCLING: ways to define	149
Talking Words	151
Blood Flow	160
Animation	166

LAYERING: ways to divide	174
Sliced Pie	175
Double Exposure	182
Thirteen Blackbirds	187

UNCORKING: ways to disarm	194
Devil's Advice	195
Mocking with Media	200
"Are You Talking to Me?"	205
Sincerely Yours	213

ABOUT THE AUTHORS

Gary Hoffman studied architecture at the University of California Berkeley before studying English and art at the University of California Los Angeles where he received his Master of Arts, then completed post-graduate work and taught English at the University of Southern California. He has taught writing and literature for over twenty-five years, and studio art for eight of those years, at Orange Coast College. He has also been a freelance landscape designer for over twenty years. Glynis Hoffman received her Masters of Arts in English at California State University at Fullerton. Before teaching she was a writing consultant and business correspondent. She has taught writing and literature in the California State University system, at several community colleges, and at the Fashion Institute of Design and Merchandising. Gary and Glynis enjoy cooking, viewing international cinema, visiting architectural sights, gardening, and reading.

ACKNOWLEDGEMENTS

Thanks for giving us our daily baguette from the La Brea Bakery; also our bread and butter, the O.C.C. English Department, and therein especially the unleavened proof-reading by the language-yeasting Donna Barnard, the grammar-kneader Robert Dees, and the word-sifter Geoffrey Bellah, who put his signed-by-E.B.-White *Elements of Style* aside; thanks to the U.C.Berkeley school of architecture's Bauhaus approach to learning the writing kitchen manifest in Gary's *Writeful,* but thanks for Glynis's muse for wanting to remix and braid that book's batter lest we heap up phrases as the teachers do; thanks to "Too Hot Tamales," Mary Sue and Susan, whom we sought, asked for bread, and received a shared-third-person-point-of-view tortilla; thanks to the editors of many major publishing houses who told us to cast our bread upon the water so that it would come back to us with *Adíos* ; thanks be to language sandwiches — Strunk & White, Scholes & Comely, Freeman now & Freeman then; and the most thanks to the essayists in Robert Atwan and Houghton-Mifflin's *Best Essays* collections, the seek-and-you-will-find writers of *Harper's Magazine*, and great language enhancers such as Henry James, Elvis Costello, Billy Faulkner, Erich Rohmer — all of whom we take, eat, for this is the body.

INTRODUCTION

The Grammar School Correction

When Gary was growing up in the 1950's and early 60's, composition instruction meant pinching content into strictly defined formats, a dry, scaly burden resulting in dead papers. There was little difference between learning writing and learning trigonometry: A student persevered through blind faith that someday the worth of both would be revealed. In the early 1970's Gary began teaching, joining the academic revolution which sought to bury the scaly, dry writing beast. This revolution recognized that many good writers broke rhetorical modes and that grammatical rules were vulnerable, fractured with regional and cultural dialects. More importantly, writing was thought to be at its best when it was inspired, mostly politically inspired, and not when wrangled into ideas of correctness. As teachers understood this, they minimized rules, so that by the mid-seventies student Glynis witnessed the unraveling of writing into a free-for-all grope of touchy-feely journals, free-writing cluster balloons, and group-talk overflows. The revolution had over-compensated for the past, so that by the 1980's writing teachers had sprouted a skills-starved beanstalk. In a panic, they chopped down subjectivity and fee-fi-fo-fummed to a "back-to-basics" tune. The dry, scaly beast was back.

By the early 1990's, graduate schools, armed with deconstruction swords, began slaying the formulaic beast all over again, this time replacing the fallen creature with "process writing," a euphemism for a form-evolves-from-necessity approach to college writing. This method relied on teachers' faith that by adhering to process, students would stumble onto the usefulness of stylistic and rhetorical modes. This faith assumed students would enthusiastically truffle-up writing skills on their own time. Playing hide-and-go-seek with established writing techniques meant leaving students little time to discover and put into action the vast potential of writing techniques. Process writing became tantamount to putting a medical student in an operating room and hoping he or she would be inventive enough to learn cutting and stitching techniques before the patient bled to death. Writing is a complicated adventure, even when a person knows helpful tools.

We think it is time that teachers get off the rules-no-rules teeter-totter and start asking themselves why, for over fifty years, students have enjoyed learning in automotive, art, music, culinary, fashion design, and physical education classes but not in writing classes. For us, the reason is clear. First, students need to be taught the tools which professional writers have tested for decades, not the ones teachers have turned into painful dogma. Also, student writers cannot be asked to accept these tools on faith but must be presented the tools in ways that are immediately accessible, appealing simultaneously to both the rational and imaginative parts of the mind. This means two things must always happen: Every tool must be presented as if it were an intriguing magic wand, appearing powerful in its own right; and when the tool is tried out, students must immediately see its ability to be a language cruncher, a solution to a stylistic or organizational problem which dramatically revives a written piece. This treatment of tools and techniques is what makes art and cooking classes so energized. Students in those disciplines are never asked to accept skills on faith, deferring usefulness into the distant future.

Learning to Write Before Learning to Read

Before taking our classes, many of our students had become entangled in the stylistic and organizational complexities of strong essays when they tried to read them. Our students become better readers of professional writers because the students have learned to recognize their tools when used by others. Learning how to use style enables students to comprehend the music and rhythms of writing, an exciting connection, a nexus similar to that made by an art student who has learned to use a palette knife in order to flutter millions of leaves, and thereafter can recognize when a great painter has used one as well. It is extremely difficult to even recognize what an artist or craftsperson is doing if one has not tried it beforehand, and it is virtually impossible to appreciate the excellence with which a stylistic device or strategic form is used if a person has never attempted using it. A person who has tried to hit a golf ball appreciates a pro's swing more than someone who has never played golf. This means that writing comes before reading every bit as much as the standard English teacher's notion that reading comes before writing.

Selecting great writers as examples for students presents another problem. The process-writing proponents of the 1990's were inherently hypocritical in that, while they placed a gag order on form and structure in favor of endless brainstorming , revising, and cluster sniffing, these same instructors, well marinated in political correctness, felt compelled to force-feed students with socio-politically correct topics, as if only these would nourish inspired writing. Too often they rejected writers who were not topical, who did not neatly lock into an easily defined category of writing, or who had a strong personal voice. The late twentieth century has been an exciting time for the essay genre which experienced a revitalization in 1986 when Houghton Mifflin began publishing a yearly selection of expository pieces in *The Best American Essays*. Professional writers started reexamining the genre and many noted fiction writers such as Jamaica Kincaid and poets like Josephine Foo became attracted to expository writing for the richness and flexibility of the genre.

What makes these essays exciting is not whether they are topical (they usually are) or that the writers are from under-represented groups, but that the writing is energized. Shelby Steele, for instance, challenges the notion of entitlements for marginalized groups by tossing out a traditional college-textbook management of the issue, instead allowing his personal experiences, voice, and a blend of rhetorical devices, some even associated with fiction, to articulate his ideas. The result is neither strictly personal nor universal, neither sociological nor literary. It is all of these. This is the kind of writer that students should be reading. A few exist in every college reader, but we call these types of essayists the Best-American-Essay writer in honor of Houghton Mifflin's efforts to promote the idea of an essay being more than something written for and read in college courses.

Neither a Trade Book Nor a Text Book Be

Our book was conceived with teachers, students, and free-lance writers in mind. It does not pretend to fit a narrowly defined target market: It is neither a committee-toned textbook nor a personalized trade book, but something in between. Many of the approaches here will appeal to elementary school teachers, others to graduate seminar professors. This pleases us because we believe that the use of this book should be a function of the teacher's personality. The idea of an instructor's manual that tries to tell teachers how to use an instructional book makes us ill. However for a fee, we will build a customized syllabus with the reader you are using in class so that your reader's essays will co-ordinate with all of the sections in *Adíos,Strunk and White*. For any questions about using this book in class, write to Gary & Glynis Hoffman, Orange Coast College, 2701 Fairview Road, Costa Mesa, CA, 92626.

We never cover all of the material here in our own classes. The section on Thought is usually the focus of only one paper, sometimes a researched analysis, although ideally it should be the central process for every paper. We use it as a constant focus in our second semester, critical thinking courses. Both of us are thorough with the Style unit, holding off on introducing only a few of the style devices until we reach an especially relevant organizational strategy. As far as the Form unit itself goes, Glynis spends more time on a few of the strategies; Gary allows students to drop some after working up rough drafts on several. The order in which the Forms of part three are introduced varies to compliment whatever types of essays a class is reading.

In 1919 William Strunk Jr. self-published his own textbook at Cornell entitled *The Elements of Style*, which he copyrighted in 1935. E .B. White was a student in that class, and in 1975, after Strunk died, White was asked by Macmillan to revise the book for both the college and general trade market. He did and kept updating the text until 1979, with reprints into the 1990's.   For most of the twentieth century, Strunk and White's *The Elements of Style* has been the touchstone for professional writers, teachers, and students. White always admired the brevity of the book and also Strunk's "kindly lash" that made the book a series of sharp commands.   Strunk and White attempted to capture the most essential elements of writing in a tightly wrapped, useful book. We like to think our book pays homage to that spirit. In other, more ideologically significant ways, we have departed from Strunk and White. Writing did too. In the last part of the twentieth century, written expression has expanded further than either Strunk or White could have dreamt of in their instructional philosophies. The rules for the twenty-first century need to be recreated and they demand new explanations, especially for a more visual-oriented, computer-literate, cyberspace-writing generation. In order to best prepare essayists for this world, we have no choice — Adíos, Strunk and White.

A Disclaimer

Any of the advice in *Adíos, Strunk & White* can be abused, misused, or followed without complete understanding. Strong writers always take calculated risks. Any writer who uses the advice in this book must practice it over and over again, constantly revising initial drafts and also being mature enough to know when to apply certain writing devices presented in this book and when not to. All writers are responsible for anything they write, no matter what advice they have received or whether they have clearly articulated their intentions. We take only partial credit or blame for the brilliance or utter crap which results from using this book.

S T Y L E

FLOW 　　　　　　　　　　　FUSION

PAUSE 　　　**1**　　　　　　SCRUB

Style Before Organization

This text begins with instruction in style techniques, the small parts of writing having to do with words and sentences. Style is usually reserved for creative writing courses or discussions about literature, yet the strongest essays must be rich with style. In some ways, sentences and individual words make more difference to a piece of writing than overall organization and the general idea. Often, when we read magazine articles, newspaper columns, short stories, letters, or memos, our memories pin the overall idea or thesis onto one or two well-put sentences and crumble away the skeletal structure of the work we have just read. Other times, we simply remember the tone of the writer's voice, created by his or her style, and that reminds us of everything we thought was important about the piece. Style is an essay's soul.

Style creates a subtext, the mysterious under-language world that informs indirectly, and since it is indirect, writing instructors have hesitated to explore style. English teachers have always taught that essays have a major point and that such a point must be supported with examples. True, but it has been misleading to pretend that writers can travel from their introduction to a conclusion only by grafting one supporting example to another. The surface of any essay appears to be doing only this, but all the content of the essay is filtered through the writer's voice or style, and when writers neglect this, the essay is reduced to a stretched skin where all the seams show. Artificiality scars conviction and meaning. Sincere depiction of reality vanishes.

For instance, in Joy Williams' essay "The Killing Game," the writer uses style to create a sarcastic voice, using prostitution metaphors and short sentences packed with incredulity and juxtaposing her own voice against the italicized, pro-hunting rhetoric of actual quotes Williams has lifted from hunting publications. This contrast renders their style unrealistic and absurd and helps to justify her abhorrence for their pro-hunting arguments. Williams knows that voice created by style reflects one's view of reality. On the surface of her essay, Williams says many good things and gives several examples of why hunting is an appalling excuse to kill, but these examples would die if they were not underscored by her style.

Since style creates a writer's voice, many feel that style cannot be taught and that the distinctive styles of essayists such as Jonathan Swift, H. L. Mencken, Annie Dillard, and so many others come from these writers' DNA. Just as when we use our talking voice and body language to make our points effective, written style is largely determined by a writer's passion, understanding, and sincerity about the subject at hand; but a written piece is a crafted work, not a spontaneous outburst, and writers can refine and develop one or more styles to capture the uniqueness of their vision.

It is now feasible and necessary to teach style in composition courses. First, word processors have made stylistic revisions much easier. Also, students no longer need to spend hours planning essays: They can go straight to writing and then rewriting, devoting much more time to gradually shaping organization and spending much more time refining style. Secondly, academic

STYLE 15

writing has changed. The idea of a single, correct academic style has become passé. Colleges and universities are now populated by students from diverse cultural backgrounds who bring their own style and sensibility to composition, so that a writer such as Amy Tan can include a whole page of her mother's "broken English" in her essay "Mother Tongue." Also, during the last half of the twentieth century, many scholars have devoted serious thought and work to "popular culture." Not only are pop, media, and consumer cultures now subjects for serious academic discourse, writers such as Camille Paglia and William Gass blend words and images from these cultures with the priestly voice of academia, thereby depicting reality with the strengths of both literary allusions and pop images. In short, the distinction between learning to write essays for college and learning to write to communicate has disappeared.

Style does not appear automatically when one writes. Regardless of the passion driving a writer's content, without using language principles, even the most noble thoughts and feelings can dissolve when they hit paper. The problem for most writing students is that the traditional grammatical rules for creating style can be overwhelming, and even when they are memorized, students are not encouraged to think of rules in terms of their emotional or psychological purposes. Students choke on rules that are not meaningful so we have done something never tried before. The style unit in this book boils many grammatical rules down, simplifies them, and melts them into concepts that are accessible to the playful and expressive parts of the mind. All writers, whether they are great fiction writers, business correspondents, scientific explorers, journalists, or restaurant critics, use these concepts. What writers do with them is governed by individual purposes and DNA, but all writers are using the same notes and color wheels we define in this unit to create their sounds and hues. Writing style depends on four major writing activities that together are the language of style: flow, pause, fusion, and scrub. The four forces constantly combine and recombine in surprising ways to create a writer's unique voice.

F L O W

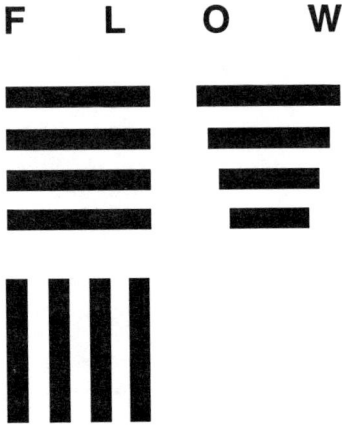

ways to speed pace
and create smoothness

Before we get to preschool we know how to say, "He throws the ball," and by the time we get out of first grade we can write, maybe with misspellings, "He throws the ball." But by first grade we can say so much more than we can write: "Bill, the guy who is always getting me in trouble and never listens to the teacher — but she always says 'He's trying,' — and John, the guy who fed the rat to Kurt, the python at school, both got sick and started throwing up all over the floor, the desks, and Mr. Skumawitz, the new principal everyone calls Skoomie." In his early years of teaching, Gary realized that even as adults we are afraid to write such long sentences and that until students were able to, they would never have the control and language scope available to professional writers. We both know that length-stunting stems

FLOW

from years of students being taught to shorten their sentences by English teachers weary from correcting length-related entanglements. Out of painful necessity, length-stunting became part of English instruction dogma.

The point is, the sentence about Bill and John needs to be long. We make it long when we speak because we know that the characters, actions, and sub-thoughts work together to create a reality that is as exhausting and fraught with sideshows as the actual event was when it happened. The sentence's length smooths reality's flow, allowing the sentence to capture the intertwined mini experiences that together create an elongated reality. If the sentence were to be shattered into smaller sentences, the reality of the experience would be compromised, if not totally lost.

Following are three methods that smooth the flow: Freighting, Telescoping, and Netting. Strong writers use all these methods to different degrees, and you will finally combine all of them to create infinite varieties of flow, resulting in different voices that serve a multitude of purposes.

FREIGHTING

Freighting involves thinking of the parts of a simple sentence as flat-bed freight cars, each one capable of having more similar material piled vertically on top of it. This material is then snapped onto the top of its appropriate freight load with commas. For instance, in the simple sentence "Bill chewed a red apple," there are essentially four freight cars: "Bill," "chewed," "red," and "apple." Freighting requires the writer to take a more careful look at the reality the sentence describes and decide what other details belong in the sentence's flow.

For example, one needs to ask whether anyone other than Bill chewed the apple. If so, they are snapped on top of the "Bill" car: "Bill, my aunt Tina, and all their cronies chewed a red apple." Next, one looks closely at reality and decides if the apple was only chewed or whether it met another fate at the characters' hands. These actions get snapped onto the "chew" freight car: "Bill, my aunt Tina, and all their cronies, chopped, chewed, and pulverized the red apple." Never stop observing. Maybe the apples were not just red, and maybe more than apples filled the food trough. Using commas, snap more material on top of the "red" and "apple" cars. The final freight train could look like this: "Bill, my aunt Tina, and all their cronies, chopped, chewed, and utterly pulverized the red, hard, juicy, candied apple, and the mud-brown, crumbling cookies, scatter-shot with chocolate chips."

Phrases attached to the main sentence may also be viewed as freight cars. For example, if the sentence above read "While opening the door, Bill chewed a red apple," it might eventually read "While opening the door, tip-toeing across the threshold, and throwing himself at his boss's mercy, Bill chewed a red apple." Realize too that your piled up items do not need to be one word entries but can be phrases, adding even more information to the flow. For instance, "Bill, my aunt Tina, and all their cronies" may weigh in as "Bill, who you can count on to sniff out the best groceries, my aunt Tina, who is a freeloader, and all their cronies, who show up only when the larder is full . . . ."

Much more can be added to all the above "apple" sentences. Sentence trains can be switched onto a second track that has its own train and, if the two are related closely in idea, they can be bolted together with connecting words such as "and," "but," "or," "besides," "because," and many others, including the semi-colon (;) that can be used with or replace some of these connectors. (See Chapter 3 on semi-colons, colons, and dashes.) The final result could read like the following: "While opening the door, tip-

FLOW

toeing across the threshold, and throwing themselves at their boss's mercy, Bill, who you can count on to sniff out the best groceries, my aunt Tina who is a freeloader, and all their cronies, who show up only when the larder is full, chopped, chewed, and utterly pulverized the red, hard, juicy, candied apple, and the mud brown, crumbling cookies, scatter-shot with chocolate chips, *but this apple event is not worth developing any further, even if it makes for a telling, graphic example of a point that could result in my writing a sentence that goes on for a page but says absolutely nothing of crucial importance.*"

SAMPLES: The taxi went up the hill, passed the light square, then on into the dark, still climbing, then leveled out onto a dark street behind St. Etienne du Mont, went smoothly down the asphalt, passed the tree and standing bus at the Place de la Contrascarpe, then turned onto the cobbles of the Rue Mouffetard. (Ernest Hemingway, *The Sun Also Rises*)

So with this reader [my mother] in mind — and in fact she did read my early drafts — I began to write stories using all the Englishes I grew up with: the English I spoke to my mother, which for lack of a better term might be described as "simple"; the English she used with me, which for lack of a better term might be described as "broken"; my translation of her Chinese, which could certainly be described as "watered down"; and what I imagined to be her translation of her Chinese if she could speak in perfect English, her internal language, and for that I sought to preserve the essence, but neither an English nor a Chinese structure.   I wanted to capture what language ability tests can never reveal: her intent, her passion, her imagery, the rhythms of her speech and the nature of her thoughts. (Amy Tan, "Mother Tongue")

Now, suddenly, we were in the hands of Man; that is, in the hands of Mom and Dad, proud in their new possession, proud because they have fulfilled their function, happy because they are supposed to be happy, cooing their first coos, which will be our first words — *coup de coude, coup de bec, coup de tête, coup de* main, *coup d'état, coup de grâce* — while we wonder why we are wet and where the next suck is coming from, or why there is so much noise when we bawl, why we are slapped and shaken, why we are expected to run on empty and not scream when stuck or cry when chafed, not shit so much, and not want what we want when we want it. (William Gass, "Exile")

English does not belong to people with virtue, or people with talent, or people who can remember very clearly the difference between a gerund and a gerundive, or people who have succeeded in imitating the affected unregional accents and measured sentences of television announcers. (Jim Quinn, *American Tongue and Cheek*)

Some [new flower varieties from one hundred million years ago] were pale unearthly night flowers intended to lure moths in the evening twilight, some among the orchids even took the shape of female spiders in order to attract wandering males, some flamed redly in the light of noon or twinkled modestly in the meadow grasses. (Loren Eisley, "How Flowers Changed the World," *The Immense Journey*)

I fought migraine then, ignored the warnings it sent, went to school and after to work in spite of it, sat through lectures in Middle English and presentations to advertisers with involuntary tears running down the right side of my face, threw up in washrooms, stumbled home by instinct, emptied ice trays onto my bed and tried to freeze the pain in my right temple, wished only for a neurosurgeon who would do a lobotomy on house call, and cursed my imagination. (Joan Didion, *The White Album*)

So descended the Lem, weird unwieldy flying machine, vehicle on stilts and never before landed, craft with a range of shifting velocities more than comparable to the difference from a racing car down to an amphibious duck, a vehicle with huge variations in speed and handling as it slowed, a vehicle to be flown for the first time in the rapidly changing field of gravity, and one-sixth gravity had never been experienced before in anything but the

FLOW 21

crudest simulations, and mascons beneath, their location unknown, their effect on moon gravity considerable, angles of vision altering all the time and never near to perfect, the weight of the vehicle reducing drastically as the fuel was consumed, and with it all, the computer guiding them, allowing them to feel all the confidence a one-eyed man can put in a blind man going down a dark alley, and when, at the moment they would take over them selves to fly it manually, a range of choices already tried in simulation but never in reality would be open between full manual and full computer. (Norman Mailer, *Of a Fire on the Moon*)

Thomas Jefferson is definitely the most interesting person to ever set forth on this earth, completing what would seem impossible for one man to do in a lifetime, including abolishing slave trade in Virginia; advocating the decimal monetary system; organizing the Northwest Territory; purchasing the Louisiana territory; officiating as the First Secretary of the State, Second Vice President, and the President of the American Philosophical Society; designing the Virginia State Capitol, University of Virginia, part of the design for Washington D.C., and his home Monticello, however the three achievements that he himself valued most highly, which he directed to be inscribed on his tombstone, stand out the most: Author of the Declaration of America Independence, author of the Statue of Virginia Religious Freedom, and Father of the University of Virginia. (Bill Singer, student)

Then she looked around the Salon and made the encompassing shrug-and-pout-and-flex-your-hands-from-the-wrist French gesture that in that context meant that the apparent absurdity of the act of fanning yourself in the cold is no more absurd than the whole enterprise of traveling to Paris to look at clothes that you will never wear, displayed on models to whom you bear no resemblance, in order to help a designer get people who will never attend shows like this to someday buy a perfume or a scarf that will give them the consoling illusion that they have a vague association with the kind of people who do attend shows like this — even though the people who attend shows like this are the kind who fan themselves against July heat that happens not to exist. (Adam Gopnik, "Couture Shock," *The New Yorker*)

WORKOUT: Write ten flow sentences, using the freighting technique, each one about a different aspect of your life: one about foods you enjoy, one about films or books that mean much to you, one about your family or work. They should each be six typed lines long and numbered; do not worry about putting them in an essay. As with the sample sentences, some freight cars should be stacked high with weighty material, other cars may be left with one item, and if you need to, use a connecting word (a conjunction) only one time per sentence to attach a related sentence train to your first train in order to sustain a longer flow.

COOL DOWN: We have found that students kink the flow when they do not pay attention to which car information is getting piled up on. Freighting is not an excuse to language scribble in a million directions. Remember, all the items on the subject car must stay together and then together share all the words on the verb car. If you spread items from different cars all over the flow, each subject taking its own verb off the freight car, you will create run-on sentences or comma splices: "Bill chewed the apple, Aunt Tina pulverized the red apple."   Bill and Aunt Tina must both stay together and share the freight car while "chewed" and "pulverized" stay together on theirs: "Bill and Aunt Tina chewed and pulverized the red apple."

TELESCOPING

Telescoping is another flow technique that demands that the writer view reality more closely. Although Gary devised this flow

FLOW

method especially for film and visual arts students to carefully examine a visual scene, Telescoping is also a schemata for zooming through the intricacies of an intellectual concept. Telescoping differs from Freighting in that there is not any vertical piling up of material. The first observation or sentence is left alone. The period at the end of that sentence is replaced by a comma which acts like a zoom lens to start the telescoping. Instead of imagining freight cars, your mind's eye acts as if it were a camera with an attached telephoto lens.

Consider the following simple sentence about an architectural experience we both enjoyed: "*We toured the Hollyhock house.*" Instead of adding more cargo to the sentence's words or freight cars, the sentence is left unfreighted. Next the writer replaces the period after "house" with a comma, the comma representing a telephoto lens zooming up closer to any detail on any of the items in the original sentence, which could be "we," "the tour," or the "Hollyhock house." If the writer decides to zoom up to the house itself, the sentence could now read "*We toured the Hollyhock house, the walls composed of many prefab, cement blocks.*"" This period may also be replaced with a comma, but now the writer may only zoom onto one of the details of the last phrase — "walls," "composed," "prefab," "cement," or "blocks" because now these details are all that remain framed by the "camera." Because the sentence has zoomed up closer to the house, the first, larger, we-toured-the-Hollyhock-house image gets cut out of the last frame, although it is still in the sentence.

Selecting "blocks" out of the last phrase for a second zoom, the writer might end up with the following sentence: "*We toured the Hollyhock house, the walls of the house composed of many prefab blocks , the blocks' abstract design cast as a hollyhock's flower, the hollyhocks being the house's dominant motif.*" The thinking behind building this sentence has worked like this: "We toured the Hollyhock house," (zoom up closer to the house) "the walls composed of many prefab blocks," (zoom up closer to the blocks), "the blocks' abstract design cast as a hollyhocks flower," (zoom up and closer to the flower and make a closing assessment) "the hollyhocks being the house's dominant motif."

At this point the writer could use a fourth comma to zoom onto a detail in the last phrase or, by using a comma and a connecting word ("and," "but," "while," "since"), the writer could "pan" over or "pull back" to another detail, or another idea, outside the domain of the last phrase. This is how telescoping connects two sentences. Then this new, outside "shot" would start over as a new sentence with its own complete verb and telescoping phrases. For instance, the sentence could read *"We toured the Hollyhock house, the walls composed of many prefab blocks, the abstract design of a hollyhocks flower cast as the blocks' dominant motif, and the very chunkiness of the blocks helped to emphasize the horizontal weight of the house, a horizontal strength reminiscent of Mayan government architecture."*

Freighting and Telescoping sentences do not have to be about physical realities; they can also describe conceptual realities. For instance, consider the sentence "Jesse decided to challenge Joseph Campbell's ideas." Replacing the period with a comma, the writer could "zoom" up on a more detailed description or analysis of this challenge. Of course, these sentences can also expand with a connecting word, such as "when" in the example below. The final result might be "Jesse decided to challenge Joseph Campbell's ideas, Jesse shuddering at Campbell's equating Buddha at rest under a tree with Jesus suffering under the crucifixion 'tree,' when in fact, the Buddha image represented contentment with the cycle of life, the productive tree creating a sharp contrast to the image of a punishing cross, an eternal symbol of suffering and betrayal."

Telescoping sentences can trap you. If the zoomed focuses are described with complete verbs, then the sentence becomes a comma splice, a series of complete sentences that should be separated with periods, but that have become spliced together with commas. To avoid this problem, make sure only one part of the sentence has a complete verb and all the phrases that zoom up have incomplete verbs. In the Jesse sentence above, the

FLOW

complete verb is "decided," and then the zoom up on Jesse uses the incomplete verb "shuddering" instead of "shudders" or "shuddered" or "was shuddering," which are all verbs that would turn the "Jesse shuddering at Campbell equating Buddha at rest . . ." phrase into a complete sentence, breaking the flow by requiring a period instead of a comma after the word "ideas." On the other hand, when using a connecting word such as "when," you must add a new complete verb. Without the connecting word "when," and with only a comma to tie the flow together, the compete verb "represent" would have to become incomplete, "representing."

SAMPLES: In a ring still stained with blood from the desperately fought heavyweight match that preceded it, Mike Tyson, World Boxing Council champion, at twenty the youngest heavyweight titleholder in boxing history, brings the fight for unification of the title to James "Bonecrusher" Smith, at thirty-three an aging athlete, and, yet more telling, the only heavyweight titleholder in boxing history to have graduated from college — but Smith will have none of it. (Joyce Carol Oates, "Blood, Neon, and Failure in the Desert," *The Profane Art*)

When the ants are massed together, all touching, exchanging bits of information held in their jaws like memoranda, they become a single animal. (Lewis Thomas, *The Medusa and the Snail: More notes on a Biology Watcher*)

If we don't "stop" the child, he develops very little sense of himself, becoming an automation, a reflex of the surface of his world playing upon his own surface. (Ernest Becker, *The Denial of Death*)

Many of the Brothers Grimm fairy tales contain violent images, a darker side to life that is usually edited out in Disney versions, resulting in a sappy stories with unambiguous views towards good and evil; I would like to see a new animator redo the stories, blending Disney cuddliness with the Grimms' original gruesomeness, Cinderella dancing with her Prince while cutsey mice dance around the mutilated, bleeding feet of the stepsisters, who were desperate enough to chop off their toes to make the shoe fit, a demand made by their mother in the original. (Cynthia Brown, student)

Now that I can have her only in memory, I see my grandmother in the several postures that were peculiar to her: standing at the wood stove on a winter morning and turning meat in a great iron skillet; sitting at the south window, bent above her bead work, and afterwards, when her vision failed, looking down for a long time into the fold of her hands; going out upon a cane, very slowly as she did when the weight of age came upon her; praying. I remember her most often at prayer. She made long, rambling prayers out of suffering and hope, having seen many things. (N. Scott Momaday, *The Way to Rainy Mountain*)

Is man at heart any different from the spider, I wonder: man thoughts, as limited as spider thoughts, contemplating now the nearest star with the threat of bringing with him the fungus rot from earth, wars, violence, the burden of a population he refuses to control, cherishing again his dream of the Adamic Eden he had pursued and lost in the green forests of America. (Loren Eisely, "The Hidden Teacher," *The Unexpected Universe*)

Chuck Close's well-manicured portrait of "Bob" is a titanic, visual, bespectacled monument, the face composed of wide, bright, sparkling eyes and a relaxed, open, ready-to-smile lips in an expression of moderate surprise, amusement, and foolhardiness, both becoming an acute, photo realistic campground for the eye, their minute shapes and colors exaggerated to create whimsical forms: slopes, canyons, peaks, craters, lakes, summits, and fault lines. (Gina Smith, student)

Sometimes, as with the flamingos and herons, Audubon's light is like light at noon on a white sand beach, picking out each grain of sand, yet still unifying the scene in an all-over, shadowless brightness. (Adam Gopnik, "Audubon's Passion")

WORKOUT: Usually writers never telescope more than once

FLOW

before they end the sentence or "pan" to another object in the sentence. However, in this work out, you will gain more confidence and control by forcing yourself to telescope on a telescope, even if you rarely telescope more than once per sentence in your essays. Pick a comfortable environment such as a landscape, restaurant, or social event and observe details of the people and physical setting. Write ten telescoping sentences, zooming at least twice onto specific details in each sentence.

Have a few of your sentences describe intellectual or emotional thoughts about the setting you are observing. Your sentences should be at least six typed lines long, but you can sometimes use connecting words. See the "cool down" for revision ideas.

COOL DOWN: Glynis realized that by having a complete phrase, followed by incomplete phrases, and therefore finally ending on one of those incomplete phrases, a rhythm takes over that gradually dissipates the impact of the sentence. This very focused detail, coupled with the incomplete phrase, sometimes destroys psychological closure. There are other options for ending telescoping sentences. One is to try moving the complete phrase to the end of the sentence. For instance, instead of writing "We toured the house, our shoes scuffing the wooden floors, each shoe mark creating an architectural sacrilege," one might write "Our shoes scuffing the wooden floors, each shoe mark creating an architectural sacrilege, we toured the house." Another approach is to join the last incomplete phrase with a complete sentence by using a connecting word. For instance, "We toured the house, our shoes scuffing the wooden floors, each shoe mark creating an architectural sacrilege, but we knew to take off our shoes the next time we visited." If the connection is "for," "and," "nor," "but", "or," "yet," "so," then consider using a semi-color (;) instead, which can replace any of these connectors if there are complete sentences on both sides of the semi-colon. We find students' fear of semi-colons irrational. Semi-colons can't hurt you. (See chapter 3, under Hieroglyphics for more explanation of their use.)

NETTING

In addition to Freighting and Telescoping, Glynis realized another important flow technique used by all writers. We call it Netting. Netting can occur inside a Freighting or Telescoping sentence or on its own; it can be all one long sentence or long sentences combined with short, incomplete sentences. Netting can be a catalog of situations, a litany of complaints or commands, or a drawer of intriguing images. Netting works by tenacity, whereby the build-up of items or images, by sheer number, combine to create a gestalt that is a complete, multi-layered composite of reality. Rap songs are netted lists. We create simple lists to trap our thoughts in our everyday lives: grocery lists, things-to-do lists, accounting of bills, guests lists, movies to see, workout routines, pro-con lists, but we forget to take advantage of listing when we write essays. Great essayists do not forget. When writers purposefully craft lists, they take advantage of two weaving concepts — specificity and juxtaposition.

Specificity: Comedy writers know the advantage of using a specific word or detail to help create rich humor. During one monologue, comedian Jerry Seinfeld satirizes and exaggerates the situation of friends who tell us to use themselves as a referral when going to their doctor: "Be sure you tell Dr. Smith I sent you." Unlike a salesperson, an ethical doctor would not give preferential treatment because of who he knows. Seinfeld satirizes such mentality, role-playing the doctor's response: "Oh, Joe sent you. We'll give you the real pills; everybody else we've just been giving Tic-Tacs." Seinfeld knows there is an advantage in naming a specific, capsule-shaped candy whose brand name is easily recognized and associated with silly gimmickry. If he used "candy" or "fake pills" instead of "Tic-Tacs," the comic charge would have

FLOW

been lost.

Using specificity means using richly detailed and non-general language to fill out reality. For instance, if you were creating a list of "things that are green," you might include "trees" on your list, but reality becomes more sharply edged if you name a particular kind of tree — a Douglas Fir. Getting even more specific, you could narrow down to a function for Douglas Firs such as Christmas trees, especially if you wanted to imply a happy holiday association. The more you close in on reality, the more specific Christmas trees become. There are white or flocked Christmas trees; so inserting a specific adjective can keep the tree green: "Christmas trees" becomes "unflocked Christmas trees." Or you can use a metaphoric adjective, which Gary calls Line-Ups (see chapter 4 on Fusion), and your list of things that are green can include a "naive Christmas tree," which metaphorically captures the idea of fresh green and an ominous sense that the Christmas holiday may be vulnerable to unsuspected human tensions.

Another way to make Netting more specific is to create a particular context, a whole descriptive phrase for each item caught in the net. On Glynis's Netting of green, she also had "limeade, jalapeños, and green burritos." Eventually she created a filled-out context which became part of the rest of the food section of the list: "Summer limeade washing down a throat scorched by jalapeños which were lurking inside a chili verde burrito." Creating a context to meld together items adds character and helps to tightly pull together some of the strands in the net.

Juxtaposition: Aside from being a favorite cheese-and-wine-party word for English teachers, juxtaposition is an important concept when Netting. Once specificity is obtained, arrangement becomes crucial. Juxtaposition is simply the concept of placing two items or images next to each other. Items need to be juxtaposed to create meaningful strands, since ultimately Netting is an attempt to bring order to a random sack of groceries. When Glynis's mother used to make out grocery lists, she would arrange items according to their sections in the supermarket: all produce bundled in a list, dairy products wired together, canned goods stacked together. Returning to the things-that-are-green list, Glynis begins by arranging the random list into sub categories. For instance, all the items which relate to food are twisted together in a cohesive string, followed by a group of green plants, trees, and insects. In order to weave these strings together into a larger strand, some green items will function as interesting transitions. For example, to seamlessly stitch the food list to the plants list, Glynis picks an item that lies somewhere between the two, such as "parsley," a leafy plant that can be eaten. Or since burrito was the last item in the food string, why not use "cilantro," then "parsley," and then "poison ivy" before moving on to larger plants? All three items together create a smooth, transitional tie.

Of course, items could be grouped together in various arrangements to create a variety of effects. For example, sometimes a writer may need a list which will create tension, surprise, or shock. What if "green burrito" was followed by "booger?" Both are green, both go well together because of the alliteration or repetition of the "bu" sound, but reading the two words next to each other is as disconcerting as seeing one while eating the other. The juxtaposition of the two words creates a sickening tension, reminding us that life can quickly turn from delight to disgust.

Often a writer is trying to create an experience that is real but seems imagined or a dream that seems real. Lists can be composed to capture these fleeting realities. For instance, in *The Diaries of Anais Nin*, Nin discovers Fez, Morocco, "a city which is an image of one's inner cities," having "the layers and secrecies of the inner life." Her Netting centers on in-out imagery in order to dissipate the line between the conscious and subconscious mind: houses are "intricately interwoven" by bridges and passageways and by shadows from lattice work "that seem to be crossing within a house." Sometimes Nin's mosaic shock-cuts the concrete with the irrational: "Mosques run into a merchant's home, shops into mosques, now you are under a trellised roof covered with rose vines, now walking in utter darkness through a tunnel, behind a donkey raw and bleeding from being beaten, and now you are on a bridge built by the Portuguese." Describing a similar exploration to Puerto Vallarta, Mexico, Nin even nets adjectives, describing birds with nouns describing musical instruments that sound like birds, blending the real and unreal: "Then the birds, vivid, loud, vigorous, talkative, whistles, cries, gossip, clarinets, and flutes." Other nets collapse the general world into the intimate: "Passive drinking in of color, the cafes, the shops, people; and the thrill of looking into open homes, open windows, open doors. An old lady in a rocking chair. Photographs on the walls. Palm leaves from last year's ritual Easter."

SAMPLES: A Netting of what it means to be alive: To see the golden sun and the azure sky, the out-stretched ocean, to walk upon the green earth, and to be lord of a thousand creatures, to look down giddy precipices or over distant flowery vales, to see the world spread out under one's finger in a map, to bring the stars near, to view the smallest insects in a microscope, to read history, and witness the revolutions of empires and the succession of generations, to hear the glory of Sidon and Tyre, of Babylon and Susa, as of a faded pageant, and to say all these were, and are now nothing, to think that we exist in such a point of time, and in such a corner of space, to be at once spectators and a part of the moving scene, to watch the return of the seasons, of spring and autumn . . . to traverse desert wildernesses, to listen to the midnight choir, to visit lighted halls, or plunge into the dungeon's gloom, or sit in crowded theaters and see life itself mocked, to feel heat and cold, pleasure and pain, right and wrong, truth and falsehood, to study the works of art and refine the sense of beauty to agony, to worship fame and to dream of immortality, to have read Shakespeare and belong to the same species as Sir Isaac Newton; to be and to do all this, and then in a moment to be nothing, to have it all snatched from one like a juggler's ball or a phantasmagoria; there is something revolting and incredible to sense in the transition, and no wonder that, aided by youth and warm blood, and the flush of enthusiasm, the mind contrives for a long time to reject it with disdain and loathing as a monstrous and improbable fiction, like a monkey on a house-top, that is loath, amidst its fine discoveries and specious antics, to be tumbled head-long into the street, and crushed to atoms, the sport and laughter of the multitude! (William Hazlitt, "On the Feeling of Immortality in Youth")

A Netting of foodstuffs: The pedagogue's mouth watered, as he looked upon this sumptuous promise of luxurious winter fare. In his devouring mind's eye, he pictured to himself every roasting-pig running about with a pudding in his belly, and an apple in his mouth: the pigeons were snugly put to bed in a comfortable pie, and tucked in with a coverlet of crust; the geese were swimming in their own gravy; and the ducks pairing cozily in dishes, like snug married couples, with a decent competency of onion sauce. In the porkers he saw carved out the future sleek side of bacon, and juicy relishing ham; not a turkey but he beheld dainty trussed up, with its gizzard under its wing, and per adventure, a necklace of savory sausages; and even bright chanticleer himself lay sprawling on his back, in a side-dish, with uplifted claws, as if craving that quarter which his chivalrous spirit disdained to ask while living. (Washington Irving, "The Legend of Sleepy Hollow")

A Netting of things that are English: And they [the English] ate so much food, violating another of those rules they taught me: do not indulge in gluttony. And the foods they ate actually: if only sometime I could eat cold cuts after theater, cold cuts of lamb and mint sauce, and Yorkshire pudding and scones, and clotted cream, and sausages that came from upcountry (imagine, "up-county"). And having troubling thoughts at twilight, a good time to have troubling thoughts, apparently; and servants who stole and left in the middle of a crisis, who were born with a limp or some other kind of deformity, not nourished properly in their mother's womb (that last part I figured out for myself; the point was, oh to have an untrustworthy servant): and wonderful cobbled streets onto which solid front doors opened; and people whose eyes were blue and who had fair skins and who smelled only of lavender, or sometimes sweet pea or primrose. And those flowers with those names: delphiniums, foxgloves, tulips, daf-

FLOW

fodils, floribunda, peonies; in bloom, a striking display, being cut and placed in large glass bowls, crystal, decorating rooms so large twenty families the size of mine could fit in comfortably but used only for passing through. And the weather was so remarkable because the rain fell gently always, only occasionally in deep gusts, and it colored the air various shades of gray, each an appealing shade for a dress to be worn when a portrait was being painted; and when it rained at twilight, wonderful things happened: people bumped into each other unexpectedly and that would lead to all sort of turns of events — a plot, the mere weather caused plots. (Jamaica Kincaid, "On Seeing England for the First Time")

A Netting of ways a husband tries to educate his wife: How had he attempted to remedy this state of comparative ignorance [in his wife]? Variously. By leaving in a conspicuous place a certain book open at a certain page: by assuming in her, when alluding explanatorily, latent knowledge: by open ridicule in her presence of some absent other's ignorant lapse. With what success had he attempted direct instruction? She followed not all, a part of the whole, gave attention with interest, comprehended with surprise, with care repeated, with greater difficulty remembered, forgot with ease, with misgiving rerembered, rerepeated with error. What system had proved more effective? Indirect suggestion implicating self-interest. (James Joyce, "Ithaca," *Ulysses*)

A Netting of things we wait for: Of course, we do not just wait for love; we wait for money, we wait for the weather to get warmer, colder, we wait for the plumber to come and fix the washing machine (he doesn't), we wait for a friend to give us the name of another plumber (she doesn't), we wait for our hair to grow, we wait for our children outside of school, we wait for their exam results, we wait for the letter that will undo all desolation, we wait for Sunday, when we sleep in or have the extra piece of toast, we wait for the crocuses to come up, then the daffodils, we wait for the estranged friend to ring or write and say, "I have forgiven you," we wait for our parents to love us even though they may be long since dead, we wait for the result of this or that medical test, we wait for the pain in the shoulder to ease, we wait for that sense of excitement that has gone underground but is not quite quenched, we wait for the novel that enthralls the way it happened when we first read *Jane Eyre* or *War and Peace*, we wait for the invitation to the country, and often when we are there, we wait for the bus or the car that will ferry us home to the city and our props, our own chairs, our own bed, our own habits. We wait for the parties we once gave that somehow had a luster that parties we now give completely lack. We wait (at least I do) for new potatoes, failing to concede that there are new potatoes all the time, but the ones I am waiting for were the ones dug on the twenty-ninth of June in Ireland that tasted (or was it imagination?) like no others. We wait to go to sleep and maybe fog ourselves with pills or soothing tapes to lull us thither. We wait for dreams, then we wait to be hauled out of our dreams and wait for dawn, the postman, tea, coffee, the first ring of the telephone, the advancing day. (Edna O'Brien, "Waiting")

A Netting of trash compactor items: The compressed bulk sat there like an ironic modern sculpture, massive, squat, mocking. I jabbed at it with the butt end of a rake and then spread the material over the concrete floor. I picked through it item by item, mass by shapeless mass, wondering why I felt guilty, a violator of privacy, uncovering intimate and perhaps shameful secrets. It was hard not to be be distracted by some of the things they'd chosen to submit to the Juggernaut appliance. But why did I feel like a household spy? Is garbage so private? Does it glow at the core with personal heat, with signs of one's deepest nature, clues to secret yearnings, humiliating flaws? What habits, fetishes, addictions, inclinations? What solitary acts, behavioral ruts? I found crayon drawings of a figure will full breasts and male genitals. There was a long piece of twine that contained a series of knots and loops. It seemed at first a random construction. Looking more closely I thought I detected a complex relationship between the size of the loops, the degree of the knots (single or double), and the intervals between knots with loops and freestanding knots. Some kind of occult geometry or symbolic festoon of obsessions. I found a banana skin with a tampon inside. Was this the dark underside of consumer consciousness? I came across a horrible clotted mass of hair, soap, ear swabs, crushed roaches, flip top rings, sterile pads smeared with pus and bacon fat, strands of frayed dental floss, fragments of ball point refills, toothpicks still displaying bits of impaled food. There was a pair of shredded undershorts with lipstick markings, perhaps a memento of the Grayview Motel. (Don Delillo, *White Noise*)

WORKOUT: In order to practice crafting a list and using the concept of specificity and juxtaposition, we have our students make a list of everything suggested by an abstract term such as hate or love. Writers will want to include not only foods, television shows, and people (both in the media and those in our lives), but also the list should include habits, mentalities, and even some shocking items. Try to write for ten minutes without stopping. You can work on specificity, making the list as detailed as possible at every stage throughout the netting process.

COOL DOWN: Working with a partner, try to combine lists using juxtaposition, arranging the items on both lists in such a way as to create drama. Also start matching up items that go together because they are related in concept, create a rhythm, or perhaps all begin with a certain sound. As you create strings, you will also be using specificity again to help details from both lists go together.

P A U S E

ways to slow pace
and give emphasis

Being able to flow, smoothing together details and thoughts that belong together to accurately depict reality, is no more important than being able to stop this flow, creating pause in order to emphasize special thoughts that otherwise would blend into larger language clusters. Pause sometimes occurs after flow, sometimes in the middle of flow. Pause tools sometimes seem easier to learn than flow techniques, but making them work is best appreciated after flow has been mastered because flow gives pause its context. There are many ways to pause. The following four pause techniques are essential because they all possess an important visual dimension and all have the ability to quickly heighten a reader's understanding or consciousness. All strong writers, whether they are business, scientific, fiction, or media

PAUSE 37

writers, use the following tools for a multitude of different effects.

VERY SHORT SENTENCES

The two to five word sentence is something we learn to write in the first grade. Later, we vaporize it. Maybe we abandon it because as we get older we associate longer sentences with having important, complicated things to write about, or perhaps by college we feel too much pressure to get all thoughts down quickly, running together masses of details from textbooks and reams of pushed-together lecture notes. In this mental environment, the short sentence is squashed. When it appears in writings, it is a surprise. It makes us stop.

Depending on its context, the very short sentence has different potentials. It can be climactic, create finality, or give emphasis to a previously mentioned item. In the midst of many flowing sentences, depending on its content, the very short sentence has the power to shock or sting. The very short sentence also can help underscore material that is describing something fast, terse, or tense.

SAMPLES: To create expectation: Feel the ball, turn it over in your hand; hold it across the seam or the other way, with the seam just to the side of your middle finger. Speculation stirs. You want to get outdoors and throw this spare and sensual object to somebody or, at the very least, watch somebody else throw it. The game has begun. (Roger Angell, *Five Seasons, a Baseball Companion*)

To be sarcastic: Camouflaged toilet paper is a must for the modern hunter, along with his Bronco and his beer. Too many hunters taking a dump in the woods with their roll of Charmin beside them were mistaken for white-tailed deer and shot. Hunters get excited. (Joy Williams, "The Killing Game," *Esquire*)

To be adamant: All the same, if a cure were found, would I take it? In a minute. I may be a cripple, but I'm only occasionally a loony and never a saint. Anyway, in my brand of theology God doesn't give bonus points for a limp. I'd take a cure; I just don't need one. A friend who also has MS startled me once by asking, "Do you ever say to yourself, 'Why me, Lord?'" "No, Michael, I don't," I told him, "because whenever I try, the only response I can think of is 'Why not?'" If I could make a cosmic deal, who would I put in my place? What in my life would I give up in exchange for sound limbs and a thrilling rush of energy? No one. Nothing. I might as well do the job myself. Now that I'm getting the hang of it. (Nancy Mairs, "On Being a Cripple," *Plaintext: Deciphering a Woman's Life*)

To stress an answer: So what is sent away when we are forced out of our homeland? Words. It is to get rid of our words that we are gotten rid of, since speech is not a piece of property which can be confiscated . . . but is the center of the self itself. (William Gass, "Exile," *Salmagundi*)

To create hopefulness: And they [white brothers] have come to realize that their freedom is inextricably bound to our freedom. We cannot walk alone. And as we walk, we must make the pledge that we shall always march ahead. We cannot turn back. (Martin Luther King, "I Have a Dream")

To upset expectations: For though I am a wholly vicious man/ Don't think I can't tell moral tales. I can! (Geoffrey Chaucer, "The Pardoner's Prologue," *The Canterbury Tales*)

To create edginess: I have neither heard nor read that a Santa Ana [wind] is due, but I know it, and almost everyone I have seen today knows it too. We know it because we feel it. The baby frets. The maid sulks. I rekindle a waning argument with the telephone company, then cut my losses and lie down, given over to whatever it is in the air. (Joan Didion, *Slouching Towards Bethlehem*)

To be ominous: Your time of decay may be distant, but it will surely come, for even the White Man whose God walked and talked with him as friend with friend, cannot be exempt from the common destiny. We may be brothers after all. We will see. (Chief Seattle, "Reply to Governor Steven")

MELTED-TOGETHER-WORDS

There are many English words that are made by melting together other words with hyphens. For instance, the words "blue" and "green" mean two different colors, but when they are melted with a hyphen into a third word, "blue-green," they are now both part of a new word and a whole new color. Years ago, Gary noticed students were never taught that strong writers often create new words, melting together words never joined together before. These words can be created as long as they function as a single word in the structure of the sentence, typically as a single word adjective, less often as a noun.

Melted-together-words, because of their uniqueness, their cleverness, and heavy content load, slow sentence flow and focus attention on their content. We always enjoy the wit these fresh words offer. Their packed material turns them into show-stoppers, focusing attention on material that might otherwise be blended away, usually by being split into two sentences. For instance, the following would normally be relegated to two sentences: "Nadia attempted two flips just before entering the water. The flips seemed real easy, but they turned out to be nightmares." If a writer wished to create more pause by focusing attention on material in the second sentence, then that sentence or phrases from it may be melted together and used as single word adjectives in the first sentence. The result could be the following: "Nadia attempted two, seemed-real-easy, turned-out-to-be-nightmare flips before entering the water."

Melted-together-words may never be melted to each other or to other words that work alone, as adjectives in the examples above, in the structure of the sentence. For instance, notice that there are no hyphens between the three adjectives "two," "seemed-real-easy," or "turned-out-to-be-nightmare," nor is there a hyphen between "nightmare" and the noun "flips," the word that all these new melted-together-words are modifying.

Some writers melt together words by using quotation marks around them. For us, using these marks becomes a guilt-ridden, I-know-this-word-does-not-really-exist signal from the writer to the reader. Unless the writer is using quotation marks to suggest their melted-together-word is a cliché, overused phrase that is not new, quotation marks should be saved for quotes. Also, always avoid using prefabricated melted-together-words such as "do-it-yourself" or "in-your-face." Phrases that have already been established as cliché phrases are too recognizable, speeding the reader up since the brain chews them up and spits them out without giving them any consideration.

SAMPLES: The experience of being the lone black in a group of whites was so familiar to me that I thought nothing of it as our trip began. But then halfway through the trip the professor casually turned to me and, in an isn't-the-world-funny sort of tone, said that he had just refused to rent an apartment in a house he owned to a "very nice" black couple because their color would "offend" the white couple who lived downstairs. (Shelby Steele, "On Being Black and Middle Class," *Commentary*)

"But excuse me, George Herbert, irregular-heart-beating, read-my-line-lipping, slipping-in-the-polls, do-nothing, deficit-raising, make-less-money-than-Millie-the-White-House-dog-last-year, Quayle-loving, sushi-puking Bush!" ranted Arsenio Hall when the White House said that Bush would be willing to go on a few talk shows, Arsenio's excepted. (Ann McDaniel and Clara Bingham, "Bush: The White House Blame Game," *Newsweek*.)

Skyway Systems is in high gear with just-in-time trucking. (Roger Neal, *Forbes Magazine*)

She couldn't recall the precise moment she began to feel resentful of the hand-shake-only good night, of the moist, cold, kiss-on-the-forehead routine, but she suddenly found herself unable to think of anything but how she could seduce him. (Olga Bloom, student)

Essentially this is a movie about Jessica Lange's spirit-of-the-prairie face. (Pauline Kael, *The New Yorker*)

In the internship year, we came very close to a divorce. Your basic doctor-in-training-meets-gorgeous-nurse-and-wants-to-leave-his-wife-and-small-baby story. (Louise De Salvo, "A Portrait of the Puttana as a Middle-Aged Woolf Scholar," *Between Women*)

This is not to say that all penises are, according to Pound's dictum, moral. Indeed, a gratuitously shocking penis, an extraneous-to-our-story penis, a hey-look-at-me-for-the-sake-of-nothing-but-me penis, however imposing, is literally immoral (that is, incompetent), because by jarring the reader from the narrative or argumentative flow into a mood of "What's this stupid penis doing here?" the author has undermined the greatest truth of his tale: i.e. our ability to immerse ourselves in it. (David Duncan, "Toxins in the Mother Tongue," *The Los Angeles Times Magazine*)

Like most daytime dramas, CBS's "Love of Life" simply sketches in a Dirty Secret, leaving the details up to our overheated steamon-the-windshield imaginations. (James Wolcott, *The Village Voice*)

HIEROGLYPHICS

How much of a pause the reader should take and whether it creates emphasis or establishes a complex relationship between ideas depends on visual codes called punctuation. Most students already have the comma (,) and the period (.) in their signal core: commas slowing writing with soft, slightly breath-catching pauses; the period being the most abrupt, long pause. In between the comma and period there are three more hieroglyphics: the colon (:), semi-colon (;), and dash (— or --). Whenever we introduce these in class, students balk with a since-this-has-to-do-with-rules-I'll-pass-on-it groan. Professional writers are dependent on these hieroglyphics, not because they want to demonstrate their command over English grammar, but because these marks act as guides, helping the reader know how to interpret the writer's music. In fact, learning to read a colon, semi-colon, and dash in a professional essay is as important as learning to use them in your own writing.

There are many rules of usage for the semi-colon, colon, and dash; here we are just concerned with using these hieroglyphics for the pause that gives writing its drama. A good place for semi-colons is to replace a connecting word such as but, or, yet, so, for, and, nor. Remember the words with the letters BOYS FAN. Here is an example: "I made a special trip to the store to buy eggs, but all the eggs were broken." "But" can be replaced by a semicolon if you want to create dramatic pause, in this case one suggesting a gasp of incredulity: "I made a special trip to the store to buy eggs; all the eggs were broken." Using a semi-colon to replace BOYS FAN is always a judgment call: Always know how it is adding a specific tone, voice , or attitude to your writing. Make sure it is the one you want.

One rule to remember. Unless connecting a list of items, the semi-colon can replace BOYS FAN only when there is a complete sentence on either side of it. In a sentence which reads "I went to the mall and bought underwear," do not replace the "and" with a semi-colon. The semi-colon works here: "I went to the mall; I bought some sexy lingerie." Also there is not a reason for the semi-colon in the first sentence; in the second one, the semicolon creates a pause that is almost a seductive glance. What starts out as an ordinary sentence becomes an enticement.

Semi-colons are also useful when you are freighting and you have a long list of items which are loaded with modifying information set off by commas: "Today, I received several packages from mail order companies: a hundred rolls of recycled, non-bleached toilet paper from Seventh Generation, an environmentally sensitive retailer; a raspberry beret to go with my navy wool suit from Tweeds in Roanoke, Virginia; a two-pound box of assorted chocolates, all soft centers, no nuts, including the scotch mallow, a dark chocolate candy filled with a layer of butterscotch and a layer of marshmallow, from See's Candies." The semicolons here are useful for keeping the items received mail-order separate from the details given about each of them.

The colon (:) is used to indicate that either examples or a restatement of the first part of the sentence will now follow in the next part of the sentence. Sometimes writers use the long dash discussed below instead of a colon. When a writer uses a colon, the writer drops transitional words or verbs to connect the first part of the sentence with the second sentence. The colon is therefore used at the end of a complete thought where a period would be allowed; then a list of examples or a restatement follows immediately and abruptly. The use of the colon, instead of a period or transitions, gives both halves of the sentence fresh emphasis.

For instance, one could write, "The colon is a magical hieroglyphic that connects the world of generalities with the world of specifics: the barnyard with chickens, cows and pigs; criminals with pickpockets, thieves, and killers; language with instruction manuals, student essays, and great works of art." The colon here has replaced the transitional phrases "such as" or "for example," phrases which would have smoothly flowed the general state ment about what colons do, together with the three examples where it might actually be used to connect a category with its specifics. The pause created by the colon does two things: It gives emphasis to the general statement about colons so that the statement does not get lost in the rest of the long sentence, and it makes the list of examples seem special in their own right rather than subservient to the general statement they support. After the colon, the listed items can be read the way they would be spoken during a role call — abruptly, almost out of nowhere.

The dash, (— or --) has become one of the most popular and versatile hieroglyphics. With the post-modern preoccupation for subtext — or ideas that are implied and not on the surface of reality or writings — and with the impulse to pay closer attention to information that was once considered mundane, without obvious worth or beside the point, writers consider it crucial to signal the reader they are entering a parallel level of reality without totally exiting the surface one. In this sense, the dash transports the reader to worlds sometimes considered parenthetical but now actually held in high esteem.

Parentheses ( ) shut items up in a closet, almost whispering to the reader that information is being divulged that perhaps should not be. For example, "Sue was not feeling well (she had the flu) but she attended the concert anyway." On the other hand, commas lower their voice even more, not at all suggesting that we are momentarily plunging into another realty any different than the one at the surface. "Sue was not feeling well, she had the flu, but she attended the concert anyway." The dash is very strong — floating the parenthetical information quickly and forcefully to the surface — but lets the reader know the surface text is being

PAUSE

interrupted for only a split second. For example, "Sue was not feeling well — she had the flu — but she attended the concert anyway." Compared to the whispers of parentheses and commas, a dash screams.

SAMPLES: Audubon saw that the behavior of birds, their instinctual code of greetings and seductions, could be recorded as affectations: the heron's dainty, bent-wristed greeting to its fellows; the red-necked grebe sapiently lecturing its child; the great horned owls staring down their accusers. Mated birds in Audubon are not slaves of instinct but married couples; they are always in cahoots. Or else his birds stand alone in fancy dress and become worldly types: the senatorial pelican, the demagogic shrike, the seigneurial blue heron, the outlaw vulture. (Adam Gopnik, "Audubon's Passion," *The New Yorker*)

Our previous definition of the human — that we reason; that we reflect upon ourselves; that we make tools; we speak — is in the shop for microchip repairs. We are really, when you count performance and tabulate behavior, not supercomputers, but a lot like locusts, little chafing dishes maybe, small woks, modest ovens, simple furnaces, barbecue pits and picnic grills: we consume. (William Gass, "Exile")

It might be argued that America's fascination with sports — if " fascination" is not too weak a word for such frenzied devotion, weekend after weekend, season after season, in the lives of the majority of men — has to do not only with the power of taboo to violate, or transcend, or render obsolete conventional categories of morality, but with the dark, denied, muted, eclipsed, and wholly unarticulated underside of America's religion of success. Sports is only partly about winning; it is also about losing. Failure, hurt, ignominy, disgrace, physical injury, sometimes even death — these are facts of life, perhaps the very bedrock of lives, which the sports-actor, or athlete, must dramatize in the flesh; and always against his will. (Joyce Carol Oates, "Blood, Neon, and Failure in the Desert," *The Profane Art*)

I have a dream that one day down in Alabama — with its vicious racists, with its Governor having his lips dripping with the words of interposition and nullification — one day right there in Alabama, little black boys and black girls will be able to join hands with little white boys and white girls as sisters and brothers. (Martin Luther King, "I Have a Dream")

Whatever my romantic notions were about the ideal forms of American Indian wisdom — closeness to the land, respect for other living creatures, a sense of harmony with natural cycles, a way of walking lightly in the world, a manner of living that could make the ordinary and profane into the sacred — I learned that on the reservation I was inhabiting a world that was contrary to all these values. (Diana Hume George, "Wounded Chevy at Wounded Knee," *The Mississippi Review*)

Lanegrin's equation for motion therefore has its roots in two worlds: the macroscopic world represented by the diagonal force and the microscopic world represented by the fluctuating, or Brownian force. (Bernard Lavends, *Scientific America*)

In the world of canned dog food, a smooth consistency is a sign of low quality — lots of cereal. A lumpy, frightening, bloody, stringy horror is a sign of high quality — lots of meat. (Ann Hodgman, "No Wonder They Call Me a Bitch," *Spy*)

Some books are to be tasted, others to be swallowed, and some few to be chewed and digested: that is, some books are to be read only in parts; others to be read, but not curiously [with great care]; and some few to be read wholly and with diligence and attention. (Francis Bacon, "Of Studies")

Life's but a walking shadow, a poor player/ That struts and frets his hour upon the stage/ And then is heard no more: it is a tale/ Told by an idiot, full of sound and fury,/ Signifying nothing. (William Shakespeare, *Macbeth*)

PAUSE

SUPER-LITERALISM

A powerful way to bring pause to a piece of writing is to reduce words or phrases to their most basic, taken-for-granted elements. This requires treating a simple word like "apple" as if it were abstract terminology, then reducing that word to an even simpler, down-to-earth reality. Super-Literalism slaps euphemisms in the face (euphemism is discussed in the Scrub chapter). Notice that in the following sentence, apple gets no more attentive pause than any of the other fruits: "I bought grapes, oranges, bananas, and apples." When Super-Literalism is used as a reducing agent, notice how the apple now receives stunning attention: "I bought grapes, oranges, bananas, and shiny red seed pods." "Shiny red seed pods" is a more truthful, graphic phrase than "apples," more truthful because "shiny red seed pods" reduces "apple" to characteristics we have taken for granted.

Super-Literalism is not metaphor: It does not compare unlike things. Describing spaghetti as slimy worms is metaphoric; describing it as dry sticks of crushed grass seed and chicken embryo is Super-literal. Super-literalism is always a shock. It reminds us that we and the world are a bit more vulnerable, animalistic, or manufactured than numb, common words allow us to believe. Super-Literalism is conscious-raising because it is a complacency shaker. The more abstract, intellectual, or sophisticated the tone of the ongoing flow in a piece of writing, the more abruptly the injection of Super-Literalism forces the reader's nose down into reality.

Gary has always been impressed by philosopher Alan Watt's use of Super-Literalism in his book *Does It Matter?* For instance, imagine an ecology or biology teacher talking about food chains, a hierarchy of predators that live by eating animals lower on a prey list. Typically, the professor would refer to this as a food web or maybe symbiotic relationships. Watt stops the reader cold though when he reduces this phenomenon to its most graphic, taken-for-granted version: ". . . almost all the substance of this maze [of life], aside from water, was once other living bodies — the bodies of animals and plant — and that I had to obtain it by murder . . . I exist solely through membership in this perfectly weird arrangement of beings that flourish by chewing each other up." "Murder," and especially "chewing each other up," reduce "food web" to an explanation a small child could understand. "Food web" or "food chain" protects the reader, distancing the reader from reality by being more abstract. "Chewing each other up" shocks us into remembering our animal selves. We cannot help but take pause. Super-Literalism punches the wind out of euphemism and makes us reconsider what we have read even more than most short sentences can.

Many so-called primitive or aboriginal tribes use language that is graphic Super-Literalism. This type of language has powerful identifying capabilities that later vanishes in industrial, scientific societies, trapped by the need to categorize or label to keep track of fine distinctions. Ruth Bebe Hill lived for over thirty years with the Lakota to learn their language before writing her novel *Hanta Yo*. Looking through the glossary of Bebe's novel is revealing. "Long-claws" is a much more descriptive name for an animal than grizzly bear. "Lump-raiser" is a name that describes a physical interaction that is taken for granted with the label "mosquito." "Bird-that-vexes-air" captures more about the relationship between the bird and its amazing manner of flight than "hummingbird."

Super-Literalism has magic that turns a reader's head. It is a powerful stun tool; it needs to be used sparingly to be effective. When a writer is aware of the possibilities of Super-Literalism, all language comes under playful scrutiny and so over-all expression becomes clearer. In some ways, no other pause tool adds as much clarity, honesty, irony, and sometimes humor, to all

PAUSE

kinds of writing — scientific, philosophical, or business — as Super-literalism does.

SAMPLES: We have put Super-literal language in italics. Some might argue that a few of these are metaphors, but given their context, we think everything here is Super-Literal.

There is no question that there is an unseen world. The problem is, *how far is it from midtown and how late is it open*? (Woody Allen, "Examining Psychic Phenomena," *The New Yorker*. For a literal-minded person, who does not see spirituality in metaphorical terms, Allen's question is literal, and therefore humorous to those who are not literal-minded.)

Gerber dismisses the Stages line as a copy of its own color-coded system, which differentiates the *mush* from the *chunks* but does not organize the food according to the baby's age. (Jaclyn Fierman, *Fortune Magazine*. Normally these foods would be referred to as strained and natural; here they are what they really look and feel like.)

I said there was a society of men among us, bred up from their youth in the art of proving by words multiplied for the purpose, that white is black and black is white, according as they are paid. To this society all the rest of the people are slaves. For example, if my neighbor hath a mind to my cow, he hires a lawyer to prove that he ought to have my cow from me. I must then hire another to defend my right, it being against all rules of law that any man should be allowed to speak for himself. . . . It is likewise to be observed that this society hath a peculiar cant and jargon of their own, that no other mortal can understand, and wherein all their laws are written, which they take special care to multiply; whereby they have wholly confounded the very essence of truth and falsehood, of right and wrong; so that it will take thirty years to decide whether the field, left me by my ancestors for six generations, belong to me or to a stranger three hundred miles off. (Jonathan Swift, "Voyage to the Houyhnhums," *Gulliver's Travels*. Maybe the whole passage should be italicized.)

In World War I [engineers] made a machine that would *throw five hundred pounds of steel fifty miles.* (Andy Rooney, "An Essay on War," *Literary Calvacade.* Super-literalism here reminds us of the gravitational limitations an artillery canon must overcome.)

In the Amazon, on the other hand, should you have had too much to drink, say, and inadvertently urinate as you swim, any home less candiru, attracted by the smell, will take you for a big fish and swim *excitedly* up your stream of uric acid, enter your urethra like a worm into its burrow, and, raising its gill cover, stick out a set of retrose spines. Nothing can be done. The pain, apparently, is spectacular. (Redmond O'Hanlon, "Amazon Adventure," *Granta.* Normally these words would be used as hyperbole or exaggeration; here they are almost understatements.)

Jones is next wheeled into the appointed slumber room where a few touches may be added — his favorite pipe placed in his hand or, if he was a great reader, a book propped into position. . . . Here he will *hold open house* for a few days, visiting hours 10 A.M. to 9 P.M. (Jessica Mitford, T*he American Way of Death.* No corpse, no open house. It really is the dead's last party.)

I am an *invisible man.* No, I am not a spook like those who haunted Edgar Alan Poe. . . . I am invisible, understand, simply because people refuse to see me. (Ralph Ellison, *Invisible Man.* For the Afro-American persona that speaks here, white people literally do not see him, in the same way a student sitting in a hallway is perceived as part of the walls by a professor who carries on a personal conversation within that student's listening range.)

As Aristotle put it, the beginning of philosophy is wonder. I am simply amazed to find myself living on a *ball of rock* that swings around an immense *spherical fire* . . . (Alan Watt, "Murder in the Kitchen," *Does It Matter?* We do live on a ball of rock that can crack, crumble, and get slammed into by other rocks. The word "earth" is a grand, more comforting term.)

I'm sick of peering at the world through false eyelashes, so every-

PAUSE

thing I see is mixed with a shadow of *bought hairs*; I'm sick of weighting my head with a *dead mane*, unable to move my neck freely, terrified of rain, or wind, of dancing too vigorously in case I seat into my *lacquered* curls. (Germaine Greer, *The Female Eunuch*. Check the ingredients for hair spray.)

F U S I O N

ways to spark interest,
fine-tune, and compress

Essentially there are two kinds of language systems that we all use — literal and metaphoric. Literal language is straight-forward, dictionary-defined language that is essential to living and survival. If we were in a burning theater and someone warned us by shouting "the evil gods have farted" or "a liquid sun tumbles over us," we would want to cut that person's tongue out and curse language forever. In an emergency, we want a literal signal: "Fire!" The other, more ambiguous warnings are from the world of metaphor, and although they are undesirable when warning others of a fire, in many other situations metaphor has the ability to depict the complexities and subtleties of reality in a way that is impossible for literal, dictionary-defined language. Only metaphoric language flash-fuses three layers of mental involvement: its originality excites the reader's interest in the subject matter; some of the metaphor's associations capture the writer's attitude towards the subject; other associations quickly capture the complexity and subtly of the literal subject that is fused to the metaphor. In short, metaphor sparks interests, fine-tunes attitude, and compresses explanations or descriptions.

For instance, describing a building on fire as "the evil gods have farted" intrigues because the phrase has never been heard before, while at the same time the speaker's attitude is implied by the reference to "gods," suggesting that the writer finds the fire to be prophetic, and the word "farted" suggests that the speaker also finds the start of the fire to be capricious or comically absurd. Aside from intriguing the reader and implying something about the speaker's attitude, a description of the fire is compressed: The fact that "gods have farted" suggests that the fire is of cosmic magnitude or size and with an enormous foul, windy back draft. The other metaphor, "a liquid sun tumbles over us," creates an entirely different concept of a fire. Again it incites interest because of its originality, but the speaker seems more awestruck than the first writer since the "sun" is a more essential, important aspect of life than a "fart." The metaphor also defines the nature of the fire differently: The idea that the intensity of the sun could liquefy makes its heat especially intense and threatening, while "tumbles over us" suggests a fire-storm that is inescapable.

Metaphors usually work on the reader quickly and intuitively. With the fire expression above, the reader or listener has an emotional and intellectual reaction where all three dimensions of the metaphor are sucked in without analyzing the metaphor the way we just have done above. Metaphors are rich, but when they are good, we almost take them for granted, usually giving homage to them only through a split-second smile before reading or listening further. Because metaphors are so multidimensional, fusing literal material to them is essential to all kinds of writing: fictional, journalistic, business, sociological, critical, theological, political and the scientific.

English teachers avoid teaching students to use metaphor for several reasons. First of all, rules cannot be cited to evaluate metaphors; their worth can only be discussed by analyzing them in the context of their use. Secondly, discovering original metaphors demands that the writer maintain a playful mind set and then a sense of correctness to evaluate their worth in a particular context. Most teachers avoid teaching craft that requires such paradoxical skills. Thirdly, textbooks and teachers do not know playful methods to generate a metaphorical vocabulary. We do.

Teachers will define metaphor, but the definition sounds like an absurd riddle or mathematical corollary: "Metaphors inform by comparing something to be understood, or to be revitalized, to a second thing that in some crucial ways is like the first thing to be understood or revitalized, but in other important ways is very different from that thing." Other teachers go no further than to define different figures of speech: personification, simile, synecdoche, metonymy, and metaphor, a general term that loops together figurative language that does not fit the other categories. Teachers know that informing through both similarities and dissimilarities makes metaphor a powerful communication tool; but more important than defining metaphors, writers need to know how to generate metaphors and practice using them. We have developed several ways to generate metaphors; however, any one method could end up creating a metaphor evolved from one of the other methods. It is important to practice all the techniques, but eventually one may work better for you than the other.

FUSION

RECYCLABLES

Slang is to adolescents what the Modern Language Association is to graduate students. Adolescent slang is shock-value metaphor created in the teen years to shrink-wrap sexual embarrassment by cartooning genitalia or styrofoaming social insecurities by making fun of outsiders. Several years ago, a survey of nostalgic college students recalled metaphors such as "wrinkled-necked pigeons," "fur burgers," and "choke my chicken." Other times adolescent slang is used to over-dramatize the grotesque such as "smells like something crawled up your ass and died," "lung cookies," or "break wind." These metaphors do not measure up to everyone's literary or moral sense of decorum, but they never have; the slang created by the great medieval English writer, Geoffrey Chaucer, to make his Bible students seem more realistic, was also raw. They took pride in telling of every opportunity to "grind their corn;" at the same time, the Wife of Bath made fun of her man's "silly instrument," especially in light of her "God's plenty." However, for a youthful audience, not haunted by adult inhibitions, slang is genuine metaphor.

The difference between slang metaphor and metaphor in general is that slang is sometimes secretive and has value within only a narrow social group. For instance, Garry Trudeau, the creator of the "Doonesbury" comic strip, once made fun of movie industry metaphor, peppering his characters' dialogue with the slang of a motion picture deal: "We're looking at a package that's going to make this town weep," "When word hits the streets, the majors will break down our doors," "Then we're talking green light? You ran it up the flagpole and the money saluted?," and "The money loved it." Even though it is insider language, slang enlivens mundane material. When a waitress says, "I need a crowd on the hoof; let them walk," she makes having to say all day "I need three rare hamburgers to go" more fun and eventful.

In the gang world, devoid of material comfort and educational advantage, creative use of slang becomes a way to achieve status. Inventive language becomes a signature for power. When a member says he's "good from the pocket, but better from the shoulders" instead of "I can use a knife, but I am better with my fists," he not only lets his group know that he is an insider who knows the code, but that he has mental energy. In Bertolucci's masterpiece *Last Tango in Paris*, slang-creating mental energy compensates for emotional and sexual impotency for Marlon Brando's character when he says, "I got a prostate like an Idaho potato, but I'm still pretty good stick."

Slang's ability to spark interest and fine-tune frays when subjected to a great deal of repetitive usage: popularity and overuse pound inventive slang into clichés. The same thing happens with other common metaphors, especially cliché *similes*, metaphors that use the word "like" or "as" to make a direct comparison. Typical clichés include "easy as pie," "stubborn as a mule," or "broken hearted," which is not a simile. These could have been religious chant to Neanderthal man, and certainly fresh surprises five hundred years ago, but now they are prefabricated phrases, already packaged and shoplifted from the language market. A writer who serves up prefab text to his reader achieves the opposite effect of strong metaphor: Instead of capturing the reader's attention and forcing the reader to rethink reality, the cliché allows the reader's brain go on a coffee break. Below we list resources for slang-creating brain fuel.

Simile-Reforming: Similes call a great deal of attention to themselves and so usually taste very artificial. Use them sparingly. If an inventive, informative one does not come to mind, try recycling a cliché simile by dropping the "as" or "like," as well as the adjective. For instance, instead of writing "The test was as easy as pie," write "The test was pie," or think of an object that is the equivalent of pie but less cliché such as "The test was cake."

FUSION   57

Exacting comparisons are always the goal. If parts of the test were easy and others were difficult, write "The test was lemon meringue," or, if the test had several parts, "The test was a seven layer cake."

Antiquing: One of Glynis's favorite flavors of recyclables is to combine Greek and Latin prefixes, suffixes, or stems with existing cliché slang. We provide our students with lists of the suffixes, bases, and prefixes. Combining English words with French, Spanish, or Italian words also works since they come with built-in Latin echoes. When our niece throws a fit for more donuts with sprinkles on top, we say "Simone suffers from Sprinklerrhea," using the common word sprinkle; then combining it with the Greek suffix "rrhea" meaning "abnormal discharge."

Thesauruscoping: We require our students to always have a Roget's Thesaurus on hand. We recommend ones that have a wide selection of choices from common slang to lofty sounding language, as opposed to those that offer few choices but define the words. By looking up synonyms in the Thesaurus and combining them with other important words or their synonyms, you can create a cast of Fusions. This was the basis for Rich Hall and Friends who wrote a book called Sniglets. Examples included "express holes," people who violate the rules for a ten-items-or-less grocery line; "cinemuck," the sticky trash on movie theater floors; "hozone," the place where one sock in every laundry load disappears. For instance, if you were writing about the people who hang out at your local coffee house, you would simply look up "coffee" and related objects in the thesaurus to find creative alternatives which could then be paired with synonyms you look up for "drinking." Instead of referring to the clientele as "coffee drinkers," you could then create new metaphors that best capture who the people really are: mud guzzlers, pastry spongers, or java-junkies.

Culturing: In order to capture the essence of a particular group, person, idea, or image, try using a cultural reference point borrowed from pop culture, high or low art, anything that is well known to your reader, then attach an ending such as "esque," "ism," "ian," to form a new word. For example, in his novel *Generation X*, Douglas Coupland includes a glossary in which television shows or other pop icons are used to create slang. Coupland explains that "Bradyism" means "A multisibling sensibility derived from having grown up in large families. A rarity in those born after approximately 1965. Symptoms of Bradyism include a facility for mind games, emotional withdrawal in situations of overcrowding, and a deeply felt need for a well defined personal space." Even numbers can be used. A common cultural reference point for everyone with a college education is Introductory Psychology 101 so Coupland comes up with "101-ism"-"the tendency to pick apart, often in minute detail, all aspects of life using half-understood pop psychology as a tool."

SAMPLES: I told the cheese eagle (astronomy professor) that I had to leave early for an appointment with my nerve diver and his spit-sucker (dentist and hygienist). (Alicia Eddy, student)

There is no mention of jalepeño peppers in the Christian Scriptures, and neither the average child nor the average televangelist can handle them. That's no reason to legislate them clean out of our *huevos rancheros*. (David Duncan, "Toxins in the Mother Tongue," *Los Angeles Times Magazine*)
For the benefit of you who are new [to deconstruction criticism], it explained that literary theorists, following the lead of Derrida, Foucault, and others, believe language in the hands of a so-called "master of words" [a great writer] is similar to . . . a car with Mr. Magoo behind the wheel. He *thinks* he knows what he's doing, but "pedestrians" (readers) see otherwise and react accordingly. (Alex Heard, "Jargonaut," *The New Republic*)

Phlegm and impatience mingle in his voice. . . He cannot see her view — the angle of his vision, the slant of her finger, makes it incomprehensible to him. His lumpy red hand plops around in the glass casing like the agitated head of a chicken outraged by the loss of its body. (Toni Morrison, *The Bluest Eye*)

FUSION

The monster's face looked like a Domino's pizza that had just been run over by a semi — those pizzas don't look too pretty even in their normal state — and even if the furious tone of its voice could be put through a sound mixer, someone would not be able to sort his snort from his retort. (Jesse Hoffman, seventh grade)

Just as raging surf forces a would-be wader out of the ocean and onto the beach, the jangled polar field lines can shove cosmic rays away from the sun and back into the outer heliosphere. (Edward Smith and Richard Marsden, "Shooting the Solar Breeze," *The Sciences.*)

The menu says the cinnamon bun is "legendary." Bunyanesque in size, it is a full meal and then some . . . . The big fry bread is split open like a clam shell and loaded with chunks and shreds of utterly scrumptious, deeply seasoned roast beef ... Nonetheless, Frito pie (known among local connoisseurs as a "stomach grenade") is one of the most beloved dishes of the real people in and around Santa Fe . . . (Jane and Michael Stern, *Roadfood*)

Whenever Nathan Shapiro regarded Eleanor Parnell, it was like looking at the transparent overlay in the *World Book Encyclopedia.* In his mind he would flip back and forth from today's deep-voiced, black-haired, chain-smoking, heavy-breasted woman in a red sheath dress or tight dungarees, gracefully working the cork from another bottle of pink California wine, to the vague, large friendly woman in plaids who had fed him year after year on Cokes and deviled-ham sandwiches, whose leaves he had raked for seven autumns now, and who still lay somewhere underneath the new Eleanor, like the skeleton of a frog beneath the bright chaos of its circulatory system. (W.S.Trow, "You Missed It," *The New Yorker*)

A Jew raised in Mormon country, Barr intended to move from the wrong side of the tracks and sit herself smack in the middle. (James Wolcott, "Roseanne Hits Home,"*The New Yorker*)

At the far end of Giotto's chapel, rank after rank of angels throng the skies. Today "angels" can be found on the Internet, where millions of disembodied cybernauts fly around in an idealized, immaterial realm. . . . On entering net space, the frail ties of the flesh are left behind. Fat, acne, bad eyes, weedy physiques and creaky joints are jettisoned. (Margaret Wertheim, "The Medieval Consolations of Cyberspace," *The Sciences*)

WORKOUT: List ten words or phrases that describe items, events, problems or kinds of people associated with a given profession or endeavor. Endeavors could include being a student, a parent, a son or daughter, or any job or athletic team. Now opposite each item in the list create a Recyclable slang words or phrases using the techniques listed above. Everything must be fresh, nothing cliché. Most of our students create phrases that are too long: After you create slang, always ask yourself if you can shorten the word or phrase so that it is easier to read and speak. Now write a short paper using at least eight of the slang words or phrases you created; if they do not read well, change them. Do not worry about explaining what they mean in the paper, but if they seem too obscure, give the reader more details about the situation you are describing so that the Recyclable metaphor will hit with more meat.

BREAK-UPS

Our composition students often ask how they can expand their vocabulary, thinking that if they only knew more words, they could think of more interesting metaphors. Creating tasty metaphors is not dependent on possessing a huge vocabulary. Glynis loves the following recipe for making metaphors because,

FUSION

aside from adding flavor to sentences, this technique adds to the writer's vocabulary pantry by simply using "what you have" to make better recipes. Break-Ups work by taking items you already know, usually represented by a noun, and breaking it into all its smaller parts and associations, also represented by nouns. All of these nouns can then be turned into verbs, changing them instantly into metaphors. A second method is to keep them as nouns, but as a noun that follows a literal noun which has a possessive "s," or follows a possessive pronoun.

The verb slot of any sentence is a good place for a metaphor to appear since verbs power and process the sentence's action: They are the sentence's cuisinart. Take any object, for instance a kitchen, and break-up this object into its separate parts or details: saucepan, refrigerator, cupboard, oven, cereal, counter top, butcher block, microwave, oil, salt, pepper, eggs, forks, knives. By taking these ordinary nouns and using them as verbs, you can create interesting images. Many of the nouns will need to change form — add an "ed" or "ing" — to function as verbs. The translations below demonstrate how much description and idea are compressed into these nouns when they are turned into metaphoric verbs.

Elfie counter-topped her ideas. (Elfie displayed her emotions in a convenient place for everyone to see and access.)
Gary microwaves his ideas, while Jesse prefers to saucepan his. (Unable to wait, Gary quickly develops and presents his ideas, often short-cutting steps, while Jesse slowly develops his ideas as he waits patiently for their results.)
Sonya refrigerated her ideas. (Sonya's ideas remained in a protected state which allowed them to keep for a long time before slowly deteriorating.)
Trevor cupboarded his ideas. (Trevor holds his ideas, using them only when he needs them, sometimes forgetting he had ever thought of them in the first place.)
By butcher-blocking her ideas, Candace received a promotion. (By forcefully redefining her larger ideas into smaller, more orderly ones, Candace was able to receive a promotion.)

62 ADIOS, STRUNK & WHITE

If verbs are a sentence's cuisinart, possessed nouns are a sentence's blender because they smooth together two items by having one belong to the other. For example, Break-Up another subject, such as a fettucini dinner, into its parts: fettucini, tomato sauce, Parmesan cheese, garlic, oregano, basil. Use these to write about other family members by placing them after a literal possessive noun.
Jack and Sy are the family's oregano and basil. (Jack and Sy make strangers notice the appealing qualities of the family's otherwise bland attributes.)
Glenn is the family's fettucini noodle. (Glenn is neither skinny nor fat. He also entangles himself into everyone's business, absorbing everything around him.)
Marianne is the family's tomato sauce. (Marianne is essential because she adds zest and consistency to the family.)
Alastair is the family's Parmesan cheese. (Alastair is clingy, but he adds sharpness to the family's opinions.)
Keefe is the family's garlic. (Keefe has a very definite, overpowering personality which can dominate and give definition to the family.)

Notice that instead of the apostrophe and an "s," possession can be expressed with a possessive pronoun (my, your, its, hers, his, their) or the words "of the." Notice, too, that Break-Ups work just as well with pronouns and proper nouns as they do with nouns: "Harriet thinks of herself as the Martha Stewart of the division, while Carol sees herself as the division's Joan of Arc. Students in the English department claim Tom to be their tweed jacket."

Finally, the most important thing to realize about these Break-Ups is that, once the reader understands the context of the sentence or essay, the possessed noun can be dropped. For instance, in the set of sentences above, once the writer establishes for the reader that the essay is about one's role in a family, the writer later might write "Glenn is a fettucine noodle and Marianne is tomato sauce; Alastair is Parmesan cheese and Keefe is garlic."

SAMPLES: [In reference to Delilah,] Samson said to the

FUSION 63

Philistines, "If you had not plowed with my heifer, you would not have found out my riddle." ("Judges," Revised Standard Version of the Bible)

The words you are reading are shrapnel from a five-thousand-year-old cultural explosion. Archaeologists and linguists now think they know where it erupted and who set it off. (David Anthony, "Shards of Speech," *The Sciences*.)

My mother almost shattered me once, with that instinct mothers have — blind, I think, in this case, but unerring nonetheless — for striking blows along the fault-lines of their children's hearts, by telling me, in an attack on my selfishness, "We all have to make allowances for you [who have MS], of course, because of the way you are." (Nancy Mairs, "On Being a Cripple," *Plaintext: Deciphering a Woman's Life*)

Seeing the woman as she was, made them remember the envy they had stored up from other times. So they chewed up the back parts of their minds and swallowed with relish. They made burning statements with questions, and killing tools out of laughs. It was mass cruelty. (Zora Neale Hurston, *Their Eyes Were Watching God*)

The tigers of wrath are wiser than the horses of instruction. (William Blake, *The Marriage Between Heaven and Hell*)

The history of a species, or any natural phenomenon that requires unbroken continuity in a world of trouble, works like a batting streak. All are games of a gambler playing against a house with infinite resources. The gambler must eventually go bust. . . . The best of us will try to live by a few simple rules: Do justly, love mercy, walk humbly with thy God, and never draw to an inside straight. (Stephen Jay Gould, "The Streak of Streaks," *Bully for Brontosaurus: Reflections in Natural History*)

Goya took their [the court painters of Madrid'] pedestrian, literal attention to flesh and materials and intensified it until it became a way of representing the world as a spot lit theater of façades and scrims. The people in his pictures have no bones or muscles; they are bags of silk and flesh, puffed up with vanity or collapsed with pain. (Adam Gopnik, "Goya Today," *The New Yorker*)

Childhood trauma may string the biochemical trip wires that can set off later explosions of violence. (Craig Ferris, "The Rage of Innocents," *The Sciences*)

Take one gruff, vulgar, immature brute and marinate in the daily, desperate, overpopulated scramble for survival among the drunk gypsy thieves and carnival con artists praying upon the road of life; saute in a cheap Chianti savored with false madonnas and forgotten virtues; roast until rigid with hostility in the oven of rejection and disapproval; and finally sprinkle with the salt of retribution born of self-hate too long a simmer. (Dick Rawe, student, "La Strada by Fellini")

[At the dentist] It is not the local pain that causes dread, but the greater pain: the loss of speech, the pinioning, the drool tides coming and washing out, the marooning of the brain. For two hours, the brain is Robinson Crusoe alone in the bone cup of the skull, peering out at faraway chrome implements and rubber-sheathed fingers and cotton cylinders red with blood, peering out but forbidden to signal for help. (Peter Freundlich, "The Crime of the Tooth: Dentistry in the Chair," *Harper's Magazine*)

WORKOUT: If you are working with a piece of writing or text you have already written and you are revising for metaphors, first identify all the nouns and verbs. Think of an object that captures the inner essence of your essay. For instance, if you are writing about how people are manipulated and pay large prices at Disneyland, then consider using the digestive system for your Break-Ups. Try anything for breaking up: a computer, car, holiday, city, film, or the human body. Using items from the one broken up object will help unify the entire piece. For a longer work, or just to explore possibilities, you may want to make two or three Break-Up lists. Try breaking up a really strange item. Sometimes

FUSION

we have our students practice this technique out of the context of anything they are writing by first inventing a sample sentence about their family, friends, or co-workers, as we did above, and then plugging in Break-Up verbs and nouns as a way to describe these people and their actions.

COOL DOWN: Our students' biggest temptation using Break-Ups in essays is a need to explain their metaphor. You must try different Break-Ups until discovering one that is understandable in the context of the sentences in the essay in which it appears. Good metaphors should take away explanation space, not add to it, since explanatory space defeats metaphoric compression. Make sure your Break-Up is not an homonym, a word that that has the same spelling or sound as another word with a different, literal meaning. For instance, suppose you broke up "bicycle" into handlebars, spokes, wheels, gears. "The politician high-geared through the debate" works well, but "The politician spoke through the debate" does not work as a metaphor at all since "spoke" can be both a noun and a literal verb. As always, avoid clichés. Worn out wiring, such as the metaphor in "Ivy put her ideas on the back burner," does not spark interest; it short-circuits interest.

LINE-UPS

Like Break-Ups, Line-Ups make use of vocabulary you already have to help formulate interesting metaphors. In their most basic form, a Line-Up metaphor is simply a metaphoric adjective, a word that modifies a person, place, or thing. For instance, if you were describing a chair in your house, you might give information about what the chair is like and call it a "leather chair" which gives literal information about chair. Suppose you wanted to describe a chair in a way that suggested that the chair was uncomfortable, and that everyone avoided sitting in that particular chair. Then you might call it a "jealous chair." By assigning an adjective that would normally accompany an animate subject, such as the emotion "jealousy," to an inanimate object, such as "chair," you capture whole new dimensions of reality that are impossible to compress with literal adjectives.

Line-Ups work with live or animate objects, such as people, by assigning adjectives to them that would normally be associated only with inanimate objects: a metallic woman, a nuclear friend, or a stuccoed prostitute. The way to test your Line-Up is to ask ask whether your metaphor can literally be true. Can a chair really be jealous? Can a woman literally be metallic? Some potential Line-Ups are too literal or can be used with both animate and inanimate nouns. Consider the phrase "stressed chair." Normally we use stress to apply to a psychological state, but stress is also frequently used as a physical state of an object, so the Line-Up potential in this case is minimized.

There are two other ways to write a Line-Up. One is to flip-flop the adjective and noun and place a "to be" verb between them. Instead of writing "a metallic woman" a writer could write "The woman is metallic." A second, sometimes even more effective way to reshape a Line-Up, is to change the adjective before the noun into a noun equivalent and use the word "of" between the two nouns. In *House made of Dawn*, N. Scott Momaday refers to "clear, cold columns of air" instead of "columned air." "Columns" more strongly suggest something majestic and ancient about the air. By replacing an adjective with a noun, the writer uses a metaphor that could also easily have been discovered through Break-Up metaphors: "air's columns" or "columns of the air."

Similes are discussed above under "Recyclables" as being an especially overt, attention-calling metaphor: "The chair is like a jealous lover." "Like" spells out the metaphor for the reader

FUSION

rather than allowing the metaphor to play out in the reader's subconscious. Always try removing "like" or "as" from similes to create a Line-Up. Think of Line-ups as confident similes. Sometimes a Line-Up metaphor can be so apt that an entire piece of writing or essay can be devoted to exploring that connection. An extended Line-Up or simile is sometimes called an *analogy* in which you show the similarity between two seemingly dissimilar objects. For instance, in Peter Schedjal's essay on "Cement," the writer brings out the dual characteristics of cement by first comparing unhardened cement to a whore, since it will "lie down for anyone," and once cement has set, Schedjal believes cement becomes adamant like Robesperre. Schedjal knows that in order to bring out the unique qualities of an ordinary, often-overlooked substance such as cement, a writer must access the metaphorical world.

SAMPLES: A chromosome, with its snaking strands of stacked nucleotides, is a microscopic Great Wall of China. (Howard Bussey, "Chain of Being," *The Sciences* , New York Academy of Sciences.)

I am firmly of the opinion that the Macintosh is Catholic and that DOS is Protestant. . . . [The Macintosh] tells the faithful how they must proceed step by step to reach — if not the Kingdom of Heaven — the moment in which their document is printed. ... [DOS] allows free interpretation of scripture, demands difficult personal decisions . . . (Umberto Eco, "La Bustina di Minerva," *L'Espresso*)

The "organization man" may be well fed, well amused and well oiled, yet he lacks a sense of identity because none of his feelings or his thoughts originates within himself; none is authentic. (Erich Fromm, "Our Way of Life Makes Us Miserable," *Saturday Evening Post*)

The interior decor bespeaks superb Roadfood : Tired wood paneling, Formica-topped tables, . . . and a Chevrolet-time clock on the wall. (Jane and Michael Stern, *Roadfood*)

Clint Eastwood is a tall, chiseled piece of lumber — a totem pole with feet. . . . he's tense and clenched, anally vigilant. (James Walcott, "Is That a Gun in Your Pocket," *Vanity Fair*)

The paintings by Robert Williams are not Tom & Jerry or Fred & Barney but more Bugs Bunny and Mighty Mouse with a bit of wartime, pin-up girls and guys that are half-human, half-Taz added here and there in an Adam-Q setting. Williams moves in and out of boyhood dangers through the "Warriors-of-Rust" painting where a not-quite-Dennis-the-Menace kid is trying to cruise on his skateboard while avoiding life's, every-day, rusty-nailed spikes. (Marie Avila, student)

WORKOUT: To practice this technique, pick a particular location: your home, job, park, supermarket. List all the items in that place and label their major characteristics, then all the people in that place, labeling them with job descriptions and physical attributes, not their names. Now change all the labels to Line-Ups. If you visualize a tall woman in the park, think of a Line-Up replacement for the adjective "tall" that captures the woman's height and also her other, more subtle characteristics: Maybe she is a skyscraper woman, which would suggest having a very bold and erect posture as well as height. However, if the woman were tall and flamboyant, a better Line-Up would be a "feathered woman;" tall and large-framed, a "glaciated woman;" tall and gawky, a "shaky-ladder lady."

FUSION

MIX MASTERS

One game-like way to create inventive metaphors, almost in spite of one's lack of imagination, involves mixing words into sentences through rules that force one of the words into becoming a metaphor. First start with at least thirty interesting words. Gary has his students come up with their own by tearing a sheet of paper into sixteen small pieces. Then he asks the students to write thirty-two words, one on each side of the scrap pieces, that list the most important things in their lives, reduced to one word unless they are titles: food items, songs, perfumes, vacation images, films and books, clothes items, work essentials, good things and bad things from past and present experiences, but all nouns. To help achieve variety, he will tell students to think of equal amounts of items they associate with the senses: touch, sound, sight, smell, taste. Every item must be a concrete thing except for three which may be abstractions, such as God, humor, anger, kindness. Other lists might require students to come up with thirty-two items they associate with engineering, art, politics, or philosophy. If this assignment anticipates a larger research paper, then the list could be with items associated with the subject of that project.

Now the class gets in groups of no more than four or five people. One student starts the game by laying out three of his or her "cards," or pieces of paper, at random. That person, and everyone else, must write a sentence using all three words, and the sentence must make metaphorical sense. It cannot be literal. Here are the rules: (1) You can change the forms of any of the words; (2) You can add as many articles as you wish (a, an, the); (3) You may add one preposition (words than denote place, such as in, over, under, near); (4) You may add any other word whatsoever, but only one such word. The rules force you to be spontaneous in the use of all the fusion techniques listed above: turning nouns into verbs, creating unusual adjectives, inventing unheard of similes.

Here are typical examples using words from a list about the student's personal life: "The sprinklers gossiped about mowed grass," the student having used "sprinklers," a life renewing childhood image from the desert; "gossip," something important to the student's present social life; and "mowed grass," a chore that had to be cranked through every weekend while the student was a teenager. The only added word here is "about." Another student employs a melted-together, line-up metaphor, writing "The mowed-grass gossip, used the sprinkler." This sentence actually has two metaphors in it since "gossip" cannot use the sprinkler, only a person who is a gossip. The extra word is "used." A third student might write "Gossip is a sprinkler on mowed grass," "is" being the extra word, "on" being the allowed preposition, "a sprinkler on mowed grass" being the metaphor that describes what gossip is.

The first student who writes a complete "legal" sentence announces this, and everyone else has sixty seconds to finish. Everyone reads his or her sentence aloud, and then the next person puts out three "cards," and the game continues around the group several times. Sometimes the sentences become reckless, but most of the time students are amazed at what they have created. This approach to creating metaphors trains writers to play, forcing them to try different words that are important to themselves personally or to a subject they are writing about. Remember that any combination of words can become metaphorical. Mix-Masters teaches you to put pressure on yourself, to be playful, to be willing to keep throwing metaphors out that do not work, and to realize that there is the potential to create metaphors out of any words.

SAMPLES & WORKOUT: The samples could be any of the sentences listed in the samples for the other techniques above,

FUSION

minus a few words because of the rules of the game. The approach above is the workout; however, Gary developed a follow-up workout that involves trying to understand the literal worth of what has been created by the above mixing "accidents." When you finally unravel one of these mix-mastered sentences, you will appreciate how efficient metaphors really are, how much material they actually compress.

Unraveling these sentences is a three-part process that is bootcamp training in how to analyze anything. For part one, simply write out the sentence. Part two, decide which words are metaphors in the sentence. Sometimes you have a choice. For instance, look again at the sentence "The sprinklers gossiped about mowed grass." If "gossiped" is the metaphor, then "sprinklers" and "mowed grass" are literal, with the word "gossip" being a metaphor describing what the sprinklers are doing to the "mowed grass." However, if "gossiped" is literal, people actually gossiped; then there are two metaphors, "sprinklers" and "mowed grass" becoming metaphors that describe who these people are.

After you decide which will be the metaphor or metaphors, and which part of the sentence will be considered literal, write down each word that is a metaphor, and opposite each one write down all the universal associations most people have when they hear or read the literal word. Do not think of the word as being a metaphor when you write these associations down and do not write down associations that are only personal to you. Also, do not anticipate step three when you do this part or you will limit the possibilities inherent in the metaphor. For instance, if "gossip" is the metaphor, then for step two you will write "gossip: whisper, secretive, usually about something personal that is untruthful or unkind, the information changes drastically as it is passed along." You will not write "my mother" as this would be a personal association, not a universal one.

Part three is the most difficult step. Now you look at both step one and two in order to write a literal sentence that replaces all the metaphors with as many words from the list in step two or, in most cases, words that parallel the words in step two. Add as many words as you need to make the list words or their parallels work and change the structure of the sentence if you need to, but do not change the sentence in any way that would wipe out the original literal part of the sentence. The translated sentence must continue to be about sprinklers doing something with mowed grass. One thing you can count on: Your final, literal, translated sentence will be much longer than the original metaphoric sentence. Remember, metaphors compress. In this case, the word "gossip" is loaded with associations.

Here is a possible translation for our sentence. "When no one could see, the faintly hissing sprinklers damaged the mowed grass, changing its appearance." There may be other translations, but they will all be about what the sprinklers did to the mowed grass. The reasoning on this translation worked by equivocating "When no one could see" with "secretive" from step two; paralleling "faintly hissing" with "whisper" from step two (You might be tempted to use "whisper" directly in the third step, but remember, no metaphors); spinning off "damage" from "usually about something personal that is untruthful or unkind" from step two; and reducing "changing its appearance" from the larger phrase "the information changes drastically as it is passed along" from step two. You do not have to use every association from step two, but try to use most of them. They are what quickly floods the subconscious mind when someone hears the metaphor. Here is how the final exercise looks when written:

step one: The sprinklers gossiped about mowed grass.
step two: gossip: secretive, whisper, usually about some thing personal that is untruthful or unkind, the information changes drastically as it is passed along.
step three: When no one could see, the faintly hissing sprinklers damaged the mowed grass, changing its appearance.

The creator of the metaphoric sentence had no idea what the

FUSION

sentence implied when he or she first playfully created it. The person probably did not think about the metaphor but had a sense of whether the sound of the total fusion of metaphor with the literal made a likable, interesting sentence or not. The "accidental" sentence sounded right because metaphors always communicate very indirectly. The key to shifting from the metaphoric world to the literal one is to explore all possible associations in step two without anticipating step three, and then to be imaginative in paralleling the associations in step two to others that work within the original, literal part of the sentence. If you can analyze these sentences, you will be close to analyzing the metaphorical implications of anything.

S C R U B

ways to purge
insincerity and anesthesia

Strong writers scrub euphemistic language out of their writing. *Euphemism* is language that substitutes agreeable or inoffensive words for ones that are considered offensive, unpleasant, painful, indelicate, frightful, embarrassing, or mundane. In short, euphemism's purpose is to make reality more important or more pleasing than it really is. Some writers are paid or encouraged not to scrub. Euphemistic clogging starts in graduate school where students are encouraged to establish priestly positions by surrounding their material with insincere jargon-haze. Lawmakers, business correspondents, newscasters, and attorneys all cloud, anesthetize, or intimidate litigants, electorate, viewers, and customers with versions of euphemisms.

SCRUB

The best way to learn to scrub euphemism is to get behind a euphemistic mask shared by a person who depends on euphemism; then pop it off. Once you recognize euphemism and understand the tricks used by those to create it, it should be purged from your writing forever, unless one of two things happen in your life: you grow so cynical that you count on subtle forms of lying to manipulate people, or you lack the energy to carefully think through ideas and articulate them. Below are three groups of euphemistic realities, some more harmful than others: Facial Pack, War Paint, and Metal Mask. To purge the evil spirits, put on each face, and for a moment, dance with it on.

FACIAL PACKS

For the most part, facial packs are harmless attempts to make unimportant, normal-but-unappetizing realities more pleasing or important than they really are. Most of us have a few minor insecurities about facing some of the mundane realities of life. For instance, no one really cares to go into details about what pours out of their intestines or where it gets poured. That place was once euphemized as the "toilet," because a toilet was where one merely used cosmetics or shaved, in other words, a place for more pleasant, perhaps vain, activities. "Toilet" went the way of all euphemisms after a long period of time: the reality which the euphemism replaces gradually seeps back in, and a new euphemism needs to be concocted. In this case, "bathroom" became a euphemism for the "toilet," but for many, that word has begun to stink; so "little girls' room," "John," or "convenience" cover the fumes.

Sex is another animal function that most humans would rather euphemize. Again, this is usually a harmless use of language softening; it depends. For instance, if two people have a great deal of affection for one another and call sex "making love," they cover up their animal desire for sex, and highlight the emotional or spiritual attraction of sex. However, if the couple have no affection for one another, but are merely using each other as a live tissue surrogate to have orgasmic satisfaction, then to describe their sex as "making love" becomes especially euphemistic, a lie used to hide their motivations from others or to fool themselves into believing their sex is meaningful.

The term "sexual intercourse" makes the act more mechanical, because multi-syllabic, Latin or Greek stemmed words sound more important to us than monosyllabic, Anglo-Saxon words such as the word "fuck." The euphemism "sexual intercourse," by removing both the animal, passionate, or spiritual associations of sex, becomes a facial pack for medical personnel who wish to perceive the act as outside the realm of both the spiritual and the animal. Even the animal can be taken out of animals, and replaced with Jane Austenalia, when guides at Sea World refer to animal sex as "courtship behavior." Sexual euphemism can even be extended into interior design. During the late 1800's, when the word "leg" was considered too meaty and had to be euphemized as "a limb," the legs of furniture had to be covered with fringe. In the commercial world, personal ads hide "sexual desires" with "warm imaginations" and pornographic films get facial packs of "adult" or "frank."

The human ego is also groomed by euphemizing jobs and professions. These euphemisms can inflate résumés or make job descriptions seem more attractive. People who stuffed dead bodies with chemicals, boxed them, and lowered them into a hole in the dirt — notice that Super-Literalism kicks dirt on euphemisms — took on a face called "undertaker" until people really imagined themselves being taken under. At that point, "undertaker" changed to "mortician." Likewise, garbage collectors upgrade to "sanitation engineers," a teenage employee who opens up an ice cream shop inflates to a "manager;" "managers" to "executives;" "executives" to "vice presidents."

SCRUB 77

Consumer products often get waxed with facial packs to make their appearance more pleasing. If a "used" car is referred to as being "previously owned" or "repossessed," subconsciously one can hope is was used much less than if it were a "used" car. A vomit bag on an airplane takes on a friendlier face if it is labeled only "for motion discomfort." "Small," "medium," and "large" genital athletic supports for men are almost always euphemized as "medium," "large," and "extra-large;" while the pentagon gets more Congressional support for toothpicks if they are hyped as "wood interdental stimulators."

Everyday, simple realities are facial-packed. How harmless these are always depends on the context. Do you make a "weak" decision and then hide it as a "compassionate" one; collect "cronies" who give you simplistic advice and then you hide them as "friends;" do you live or work with a group "wracked with dissension" and hide it with a "healthy difference of opinion"? We find many family and work related discussions are focused on the seriousness of euphemisms. So did Leo Braudy, a member of a Dean's Search Committee at the University of Southern California, who according to *Harper's Magazine*, once warned his fellow members to be skeptical of the following soft euphemisms found in letters of recommendation for candidates requesting teaching positions: "charismatic" replaces "no interest in any opinion but his own;" "committed to the university" means "appears at every cocktail party;" "consults with faculty" neutralizes "indecisive;" "internationally known" hypes up "likes to go to or manage conferences;" "listens well" facial packs "has no ideas of his or her own." Facial packs can help people get through many painful days and cover for small sins, but they can also cover up serious professional, political, or moral dilemmas that require more truthful thought.

WORKOUT: To dramatize how much we depend on euphemisms, make a list of all your nasty habits as a student, or your flaws as a parent or child, or your shortcomings as a mate, or your inadequacies as an employee. Be sure that you list about ten or fifteen of your solidly unattractive qualities. Then for each of the flaws on your list, think of a euphemistic word or phrase which puts a prettier face on each item. For instance, if one of your student flaws is that you procrastinate, you might doll up your fault by saying you are "spontaneous" or that you have "a unique sense of time." What you want to avoid is creating antonyms, or terms which simply mean the exact opposite. Remember, the purpose of euphemism is to distort reality, and in the case of Facial Packs, the idea is to make real unpleasantries more pleasing; so in coming up with euphemisms for your flaws, you want to retain the basic flaw, but with willfully misleading language that makes a fault seem to be a virtue.

COOL DOWN: Now pretend you are working for a public relations firm and write a ten line classified advertisement trying to sell yourself to your professors, your parents, your children, your mate, or your employer. If you feel you are among the blessed and without faults, then write a flaw list of your instructor, your parents, your children, your employer, even a famous person, and then write a Facial Pack for that person.

METAL MASK

When euphemisms move from every-day world usage to describing official business, academic, governmental, social, or other professional truths and experiences, they harden into metal mask. Metal mask is also referred to as jargon, buzz words, and official labels. Instead of making language more lively or reality more accurate as metaphoric slang can, jargon sterilizes life by protecting the reader from something complex that deserves more thought or explanation. A metal masked writer cuts himself or herself off from the reader and cuts the reader off from reality.

SCRUB

All professional, governmental, and academic endeavors have their own hypnotic language chanted by their own expert metal maskers. They believe that jargon-face is necessary because it both hypes and simplifies discussion by dissolving complexity into a single, important sounding code word. Here is a typical complexity that gets metal-masked: There are people who live in demolished buildings; whose schools are a mess and whose English is almost unrecognizable; who are resentful of people who have money, but who have little chance of ever making substantial amounts of money themselves unless they do it illegally though murder, robbery, drug sales or legitimate back breaking work; who are treated as less than human because of the pigment of their skin. A neutral-sounding, official metal mask word or phrase — "disadvantaged," "underprivileged," or "culturally deprived" — can sedate the pain of these details. This is dangerous because metal mask protects a jury member, researcher, official, or lawmaker from mentioning, and eventually from even thinking about, the details of the experience the metal mask labels.

George Orwell was one of the first to pull the disguise off jargon used to mask military atrocities. For instance, during different wars of this century, waged by different countries with different ideologies, metal masks have been used to numb the effects of war's horrors on both the soldiers that wage those wars and the public that must support them. For instance, when defenseless villages have been bombarded from the air, inhabitants driven from their homes, livestock machine-gunned, grain supplies torched, women raped, and children murdered, the official anesthesia is jargon such as "pacification" or "neutralization." When innocent people are killed as scapegoats to build unification through hate, jargon such as "elimination of unreliable elements" numbs to make it easier to kill; when troops kill their own troops, the stupidity and pain is camouflaged with "friendly fire" or "incontinent ordinance."

Metal Mask goes to war everywhere, even at entertainment centers. The war on truth takes the form of an official language-mist at places such as Sea World in Orlando, Florida, where, according to the *Orlando Sentinel* a few years ago, tour guides first were required to be guided by language-numbing manuals. The guides learned to replace realities such as "hurt," "captured," "cage," and "captivity" with "injured," "acquired," "enclosure," and "controlled environment." When it is time for management at an amusement park to fire employees, management goes to its own official manual. The painful reality of "firing" is replaced with "right-sizing," "redundancy elimination," "career assessment and reemployment," or "involuntary separation."

All industries use jargon to hide dangerous or unpleasant realities from employees and the public. The atomic energy industry sedates us with "energetic disassembles" and "plutonium taking up residence," as if a good neighbor moved in when radiation leaks and spreads cancerous poison; the lumber industry "manages standing inventory through regeneration cutting" instead of logging live trees through clear cutting; the medical industry pulls sheets over eyes with "therapeutic misadventure" when someone dies on the surgery table; and the airlines evaporate responsibility for an airline explosion by referring to it as "involuntary conversion." Government softens tax bites by muzzling them with "revenue enhancements" and the Environmental Protection Agency neutralizes acid rain as "poorly buffered precipitation."

The humanities arena has its own tournaments where metal masking jousts with reality. When jargon such as "semiotic discourses," "symbolic registers," "experimental anti-myths," "formalistic breakdowns," "derivative from the deconstruction of _____ (fill in with any famous writer or artist)," or "psycholinguistic truths" trot out as weapons, two dangerous things happen. First of all, Metal Mask numbs the listener and reader and declares that, even though art is special and breaks from the ordinary, the understanding of that art can only be articulated with inflated language outside of everyday reality. Secondly, the metal mask labels replace the details of the art or literary work itself. For instance, if a literature course fills with metal mask, the authors' senses of humor, irony, moral dilemmas, and characters'

SCRUB 81

sensibilities begin to fade and lose importance. Metal-Masking the language to talk about literature cannibalizes the literature itself. The murder of great art is not as horrifying as the murder of people, but it is still painful.

One reason teachers have stopped discussing jargon and labels is because of political correctness. Social planners, leaders of support groups, and teachers started covering realities with metal mask in order to mitigate the stigma associated with racial, cultural, medical, emotional, and intellectual minorities. Metal mask created out of good intentions has the same problems with metal mask created out of negative intentions. For instance, in an article "The New Verbal Order," for *U.S. News & World Report*, John Leo points to teachers in Philadelphia creating a support group for disabled students, inflating the word "disabled" into "special needs," only to attract a homeless person who had a "special need" for housing. Then they tried "physically challenged," only to bring in a frightened fifth-grade teacher intimidated by "physically" rowdy students.

Trying to make unpleasant problems more pleasant actually confuses comprehending what the problem is in the first place. In the brothers Grimm tale "Snow White and the Seven Dwarfs," the dwarfs are small adults, considered misshapen by the upper class, and so are social outsiders. Snow White's humbling herself by cleaning their house makes her humanity credible. On the other hand, Disney's Snow White cleans for goo-goo, muffin-faced, stuffed dolls with sentimental names. This cutsey clientele turns her cleaning into a doll-house, little-girl activity that has nothing to do with the humbling that builds character in the original Grimm's tale. Disney damages the moral quality of the story when he visually euphemizes dwarfs so that they look more like toys for the normal proportioned society to which Snow White belongs. Social planners help wipe out the same reality when they change "Snow White and the Seven Dwarfs" to John Leo's parody, "One of the Monocultural Oppressed Womyn Confronts the Vertically Challenged."

82 ADIOS, STRUNK & WHITE

WORKOUT: Not only do college courses and manuals become clogged with metal mask, this jargon begins to need its own classes to explain itself. Metal mask creates layers of meaning that take time to peel away. The price for such hyped up reality is that what could have been taught in two weeks needs to be stretched into a semester. To purge this mentality, create your own metal masked course by giving instructions on a simple procedure — washing your face, throwing out the trash, giving someone a kiss— by breaking the procedure into six, numbered steps and by giving each step its own jargoned label. Create your own labels by using your thesaurus and thinking in terms of long, multi-syllabic words. Title your subject, and any of its "parts," with original metal mask.

For instance, years ago J.Robertson and G.Osborne did a similar assignment for *Datamation Magazine*. They gave directions on how to use a "Postal System Input Buffer Device," in plain English, a mailbox. They broke dropping letters into a mailbox into several paragraphs of instructions, each one labeled with metal mask: "Position of Operator," "Initial Setup," "Start Operations," "Feed Cycles." These steps were sprinkled with parenthetical "notes" and "warnings" and reference to parts that were hyped into "multi-function control lever," "but gate," "box memory."

SCRUB 83

WAR PAINT

War Paint gathers together facial packs and metal masks, stirs in a redundancy of words, and grinds up distinctions between Anglo-Saxon and Latin based words. This paste paints over a larger surface of writing than Metal Mask, replacing vivid, thoughtful writing with confusions that sound impressive and intimidating. War paint is sometimes brushed over professor's lectures, legal papers, law books, business correspondence, and speeches of the self-important. As with Facial Packs, and especially Metal Mask, War Paint relies on multi-syllablic English that has Latin and Greek origins as opposed to the often simpler Anglo-Saxon based, one syllable words. The fact that English is made up from both bases makes English a rich, exacting language that can differentiate between fine shades of meaning. War paint abuses that richness.

For instance, "said" is an Anglo-Saxon based word that means something very different from the Latin based word "indicated," a word that derives from the Latin word for "say" or "speak." Since we have both, over the centuries English has assigned a special meaning to "indicated," which implies a response that is less committed, or less direct, or more vague than "said." In fact, "indicated" can even suggest affirmation through lifted eyebrows as opposed to the directness of speech: "When we asked the instructor if homework was due tomorrow, she raised her eyebrows and grimaced, indicating that we should get it done, but she never said we must do it." Someone putting on war paint abuses this difference. For instance, if the teacher "told" the class to do their homework, it would be painting over the truth to say she "implied" that the class do their homework. That is exactly what war paint does. It uses a closely related, multi-syllabic Greek or Latin based word in place of a more accurate monosyllabic Anglo-Saxon word in order to sound more impressive and to create confusion. In the case of the teacher example, that confusion is used to make being told to do homework ambiguous and then avoid responsibility for doing it.

Avoiding responsibility is a big part of war paint. For instance, when an attorney or business correspondent for an automobile manufacturer must admit in a recall letter to a customer that the company's poor manufacturing might kill the customer driver, a palette of war paint is immediately applied. The admission is made, but it is crafted to sound intimidating and beyond reproach, while at the same time the reality of the dangerous situation is flattened through confusion. The result is designed to quiet the customer's outrage and also shift the blame away from the manufacturer. The war paint could look like this: "Please bring your car in for service. A certain deficiency could adversely affect vehicle control." The multi-syllabic word "deficiency," that normally implies "a slight lacking," paints over the truth of "poor manufacturing." Meanwhile "adversely affect vehicle control" glazes over "the car could crash, killing you." Some call this war paint professional writing; it is nothing but distortion.

Every student has one time or another tried to make up for lack of knowledge through redundancy of words. Likewise, lawmakers try to please everyone by loading laws with enough chaos for people on opposite political sides to both claim victory. Here is some layering of war paint from the Congressional Record : "The oil price structure should give the President a substantial measure of administrative flexibility to craft the price regulatory mechanism in a manner designed to optimize production form domestic properties subject to a statutory parameter requiring the regulatory pattern to proven prices from exceeding a maximum weighted average." A previous president of the National Council of Teachers of English scrubbed this statement to find "Congress should authorize the President to design an oil price structure. The system must encourage domestic production, but outlaw exorbitant prices."

SCRUB 85

Unfortunately, humanities professors, including English teachers, are sometimes guilty of war paint. Several years ago Gary wrote to art history professors throughout the University of California system asking for the title of their favorite, insightful essay about any art from anytime in history, but asking that the essay had to be free of jargon and other war paint characteristics that get in the way of clear writing. The only response was from an art history professor recommending three articles she wrote and adding, "I can't promise you these are free of jargon, as you put it, since I am committed to examining cultural products and discourses of art history and criticism from a feminist and largely poststructuralist point of view."

Descriptions of graduate literature courses can be even worse. Here is a line from one at a University of California campus: "If persons are answerable for the characters they construct when they as much as think about a person, writers of stories are no less answerable for their characters — the standard disclaimer about the resemblances between characters and persons being 'purely coincidental': notwithstanding." Is this saying "All people, including writers, sometimes consciously and sometimes accidentally, imagine characters based on people they know"? Alex Heard, writing for *The New Republic*, discovered the following phrases at a Modern Language Association convention, all designed to "obliterate the layman": "derivation from the deconstruction of Kantian formalism," "the shift from expressive to structured totality cannot *ground* mediation," and "History can be totalized when being reified only if it moves into the absence of the real."

There are two informal logical fallacies, or ways to cheat in an argument, that are closely related to war paint. Instead of painting over simple language, these fallacies involve using words that camouflage themselves. One is called *equivocation*, using a word two different ways in an argument and pretending not to. For instance, one might argue that "it is bad to learn how to critically argue because to get along in the world we need to do more good deeds and argue less." Here the word "argue" is first being used to denote a rational process with which to discover truth; second, to imply needless, irrational pugnacity. However, the writer is pretending that the stem "argue" means the same thing both times. The fallacy called *begging the question* does the opposite of equivocation. Instead of writing the same word twice as in equivocation, the word or phrase becomes a quick-change artist by appearing two times disguised in different language costumes, but really meaning the same thing each time on the claim stage. For instance, to argue that "Sexually explicit literature is objectionable because it is immoral," really claims "Sexually explicit literature is negative because it is negative." This writer is using different abstract words, "objectionable" and "immoral" as if they carry different meanings, in order to disguise a circular statement that repeats its claim instead of giving a reason for a claim.

WORKOUT: One way to demask war paint, purging it and also being able to see through the fabrications of others who use it, is to rewrite a simple adage, nursery line, or a well known quotation into war paint so that it extends a few lines over almost a third of a page. Here are some ways to do this: First, change all simple words to more complicated ones, and use as many words for each word as you can find. Second, take simple items and actions and break them into smaller unnecessary-to-talk-about parts, and use more words to discuss these. "The grass is always greener on the other side of the fence" becomes "The growth of minute, macilent leaves consistently and invariably exists in a more stimulating propagation, and in a higher realm of verdant hue or vibrant chlorophyll on the territory and confines antipodal to the separating barrier that is hued from heavily vegetated terrain and then fabricated for use of property definition." Notice that the word "fence" is broken down into its functions, "separating barrier" and "property definition," and where its material comes from, "heavily vegetated terrain," and how that material is obtained, "hued." All of these items are pumped up with facial pack and metal mask and expanded.

COOL DOWN: Aside from blown-up words and wordiness,

SCRUB

over-use of the verb "to be," having the subject of the sentence acted upon instead of doing the action, adds to war paint. This is called the *passive voice*. For instance, if "Mary had a little lamb as white as snow" is changed to "It is known Mary had a little lamb," "It is known" makes Mary seem especially important, known to many people. Likewise, if "A little lamb was given to Mary," whereby the lamb is acted upon instead of Mary acting on or having the lamb, the little lamb puffs up into a more special item than the original lines intended. This passive voice or weakened verb, sometimes combined with it-phrases, creates subtle war paint, adding just enough color to the mask's nose to lift it slightly higher in the air.

THOUGHT

PEEL   PRESS

2

FILTER

Cracking Humpty Dumpty

Having finished the Style unit, if you are in an imaginative, inventive mental state you may want to skip to the Form unit and save this unit when your analytical, argumentative self wants to grind. Whereas Style makes up the tools by which writers capture, refine, and give strength to details, deciding which details to consider in the first place and what to think and write about those details forms another immense dimension of writing. Whatever an essayist writes about — a business proposal or legalities; a work of visual, performing, gourmet or literary art; histories or political events; science or engineering; virtually anything — the essayist must first become a thinker who unpeels reality to discover a truth, and then a writer who articulates that truth to a reader who previously had not perceived it.

For the essayist-thinker, being open to discovery and being honest about findings take intellectual endurance and emotional strength. In fact, many people, afraid to explore, simply lock in their preexisting ideas as ultimate truths, securing them with the belief that they are correct until others have proved them wrong. These people turn their back on writing as discovery. When they finally do defend their beliefs, they might even argue the beliefs are valid because they have not been proven wrong, a thinking

THOUGHT

fallacy known as *ad ignoratum*, or shifting the burden of truth. Strong writers are strong thinkers who write because they want the burden of proof to be theirs even though they realize that the truth can be in flux. Sometimes, in both real or even fictional life, all the evidence needed to know truth is unavailable, but eventually it appears and modifies the truth.

After the essayist thinks through a discovery, he or she makes this revelation of truth credible in an *argument*. An argument makes a *claim* that one or more of the following types of truth exists: What something is or is not, known as a definition claim; that something resembles or does not resemble something else, known as a resemblance claim; that something is better or worse than something else, known as an evaluation claim; that something causes something else to come about, known as a causal claim; that something should or should not be implemented, known as a proposal claim. These can all be directly or indirectly stated and supported depending on what form the written piece takes. Several possibilities for form are discussed in unit 3 on Form.

In any argument, three processes are essential in revealing, testing, and expressing the truth: "Peel" offers some ways to open details to discover their worth; "Press" explains some possible ways to check and explore the worth of those details; and "Filter" demonstrates how to articulate the connections between a detail and its worth or implications. All essays employ a degree of all these elements. Some of our favorite, dramatic examples of making aspects of all three processes work together are listed at the end of this unit.

P E E L

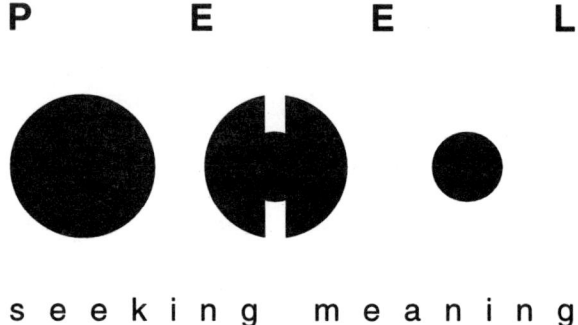

seeking meaning

"Nay, it is. I know not 'seems'" is one of Hamlet's knife-like lines in Shakespeare's famous drama *Hamlet, Prince of Denmark*. In the play, through both reason and intuition, Hamlet tries desperately to cut through the appearance of what *seems* to be true, to what is true. Hamlet's struggle is every good writer's struggle. If truth were transparent, most of the need to write would disappear: everyone would agree on which economic and business venture to follow, works of artistic merit would be immediately understood, legal issues would move quickly to conclusions, personal feelings and intentions would never result in discord, and history would never leave mysteries. Real life is more complex. People who think it is not, who try to simplify reality by ignoring complexity and ambiguity, do not become strong writers.

People who are determined to argue when they do not have an argument often become *red herring* masters, a term that refers to pretending to be a careful thinker by diverting the difficult issue at hand to an irrelevant issue that has more emotional appeal or is simpler to argue. For instance, instead of exploring a fictional character's more subtle thinking and manipulations, a critic might focus only on obvious, dramatic actions, or their absence, and pretend that this should be the center of interest. Truth is always difficult to discover because it is obscured by a truth seeker's self-deception and bias, by the intentional deception of others, and the complexity and ambiguity of truth itself. Peeling the truth before serving it is the necessary first step to every good argument.

INDUCTIVE ANALYSIS

One way to prevent being confused by "seems" or being dazzled and overwhelmed by surface deceptions and complexities is to break the situation surrounding the truth into its details, carefully considering each detail after it has been separated from the total situation being investigated. This is called *analysis*. Trying to consider any situation in its entirety, whether it be a relationship, business merger, film analysis, political candidate, or a machine, deepens the risk of ignoring crucial details that might change the viewer's perception of the situation's meaning or worth. Grasping the entirety of the situation in one gulp also tempts the essayist to desperately jump to easy, simplified conclusions about the truth.

However, gathering details can be illusive. In observing any situation, whether it be a personal, legal, political, verbal, visual or any other experience, details play peek-a-boo. We observe them; then we lose them. The mind can consider only so many at one glance. When we observe a person, political situation, painting, novel, absolutely anything, and then try to form an opinion about this situation, our minds, always easily distracted, begin to wonder if we really did notice certain details or whether those details mattered. Therefore it is virtually impossible to begin writing an essay without careful observation of details, writing each one down so that each is isolated from the others and can be thought about in its own right, giving our minds room to fully concentrate and observe new details without being distracted by the complex maze that makes up the whole.

The more details we observe, the more complete our picture of the truth becomes. Logicians say this statement is based on a *generalization warrant*, which is the assumption that it is possible to derive a general principle from a series of examples. However, collecting details is only the first part of discovering truth. Every detail has literal, denotative significance as well as implied, connotative meaning. Often it is tempting to believe that life is simple and that details have only literal significance or surface meaning. For instance, some people look at a garden and are aware of "green plants," nothing else. Literally, a garden is not much else. Others look at the same garden and think "peaceful respite from work" because their mind quickly, almost subconsciously, breaks plants into their elements — green, shade, oxygen, freshness — and thinks about the positive implications of these elements. On further reflection, these viewers may even refine those implications further, taking into consideration aspects of the garden's design and the types of plants used. For instance, if these garden details create a traditional Japanese garden, these viewers would begin to consider the implications associated with Japanese gardens, ideas having to do with Zen meditation, and philosophies having to do with the worth of existence and one's place in the universe.

You can get through life without being so aware. However, strong essayists know that all details have meaning and that the more details considered, the more meaning becomes refined. When confronted by a picture of a baby taking a bath, a person of the Western world may see the image as implying cleanliness, since babies and water are both details which imply rejuvenation. But as the anthropologist Edward Hall points out in his article, "The Anthropology of Manner," women in India are visibly offended when shown such an image. They take one more detail into consideration and think about its implications: The water is still, not moving. They wonder "how could people bathe a child in stagnant water." Writing always has to do with making an audience more aware than they were before, and that means showing readers new details as well as new implications.

By looking at enough details, allowing each detail's importance to come through before coming to a general overall conclusion of the situation being observed, the essayist becomes an *inductive* thinker. Before writing, the essayist does not start with a general idea, but instead withholds judgment, whether deciding on the worth of a work of art, a business deal, a scientific study, or a personal relationship. Inductive thinking allows for the most original and insightful opinions because the truth, plan of action, or thesis statement is gradually discovered. This way the truth is a culmination of details and implications found at the end of a journey; truth is not a precept, agenda, or itinerary that sets the direction of the journey in its beginnings.

When an essayist writes a piece, the overall truth is often called a *thesis statement* . It can end up being implied throughout the entire piece, restated and supported throughout the piece, or stated only once at the beginning, end, or in the middle of the piece. Most English composition instructors require students to state the thesis in the introductory paragraph. However, the thesis statements in a sampling of essays from the yearly *Best American Essays* will be found in a variety of places and in different forms. Wherever it occurs, the most original and insightful opinion or thesis is the result of inductive thinking, whether the thesis helps the reader understand what something is; whether or not something should be implemented; whether something is the same, not the same, better, or worse than something else; whether something causes something else. The key element is that all the observed, relevant details are clearly connected to their implications, and all the implications are finally synthesized or clustered together so that they support the essay's thesis or sometimes, several theses. (Ways to make these connections are explained under Filter below.)

A good short example of an inductive analysis is "*The* Eiffel Tower" by Roland Barthes in The *Eiffel Tower and Other Mythologies*. It is a careful, academic exploration of the implications of the Eiffel Tower. Barth demonstrates how the tower gradually moved from practical purposes to a universal symbol of Paris and finally even to a symbol of other things since it "touches the most general human image-repertoire" by implying "science of the nineteenth century, rocket, stem, derrick, phallus, lightning rod, insect."

On the other hand, what makes "Curtain Raiser," a chapter in Garrett Mattingly's historical account,The *Armada*, a special lesson in inductive thinking is that he dramatizes the implications of an event about a person who is dramatizing the implications of an event's details. The person is Mary Queen of Scots at the time of her own beheading. She turns her own death chop into an artistic drama because she knows that the treatment of her trial's details can establish her as a martyr instead of a criminal. She designs and paints the day of her own execution by wearing the red garments associated with martyrdom in paintings, by resting one hand on her escorting officer's sleeve, by raising her crucifixion high and praying for forgiveness over the sentencing voices of her executioners, and by pinning her kerchief to her auburn wig so that after the "dull chunk of the axe" when the executioner raises her head to the cry of "Long live the queen!" both come off in his hand, allowing her head, with "shrunken and withered and gray" stubble on a shiny skull, to pull off and roll on the platform, a shriveled humiliation that could only invoke pity for her and her cause.

ECLIPSE

Understanding implications calls on bringing together sensitivity, life experience, education, and imagination, all bounded by reason. Unfortunately, there are many ways this understanding can be eclipsed. One is having a cooked head, a mind that is already decided or biased; the other by having a raw head, a mind lacking in maturity or intuition.

Cooked Heads: These thinkers are those hard boiled by assumptions and prejudices, self-eclipses called *unwarranted assumptions*. A made-my-mind-up-before-I-thought-about-it writer is often someone who is a mental sloth; other times someone who is either arrogant or insecure, believing his or her life, culture, philosophy, politics, or god is better than everyone else's and so is threatened by new information that might complicate or change these views. Also, this person tends to judge the worth of unique details by shoving them into familiar, general notions that may be true in other situations, but not about the one at hand, a thinking fallacy known as a *misapplied generalization*. At best, a cooked head rots in cliché.

A version of unwarranted assumption occurs when someone's jealousy for another person is unfounded. No matter what information contradicts the jealous person's suspicions, that information is distorted by the jealous person's passion to gather support for reasons to be jealous. Even a sincerely kind act on the suspected person's part is interpreted as an attempt to cover up misdeeds. Also, maybe someone's kind acts are really not sincere, but maybe they are meant to flatter; to assume flattery is always a fingerprint for betrayal would be a misapplied generalization. For instance, flattery could simply be a weak attempt to gain emotional approval. A typical academic unwarranted assumption might involve reactions to the Brothers Grimm's fairy tales. Before rereading the originals, many people, biased by Disney versions, assumed that women play primarily passive roles in the original tales, and sentimentalists, also biased by Disney, were sure that the tales expressed unambiguous allegories of good over evil. When a reading of the original tales reveals details that disprove both assumptions, cooked heads tend to either dismiss the tales on other grounds, such as objecting to their use of the grotesque, or notice only selected tales that support their point.

Perceiving and articulating different versions of cooked heads can lead to good inductive essays. For instance, José Knighton, a poet and explorer who wrote "Eco-Porn and the Manipulation of Desire" for *Wild Earth* reprinted in *Harper's Magazine* , demonstrates how we are seduced away from the subtle beauty and essential life forms in nature because our minds are prejudiced by dramatic nature photography. For Knighton, our love affair with dramatic landscape photography becomes a reflection of our moral sensibility via our visual consciousness. He points out the danger of our desire for beautiful, light-shadow drenched landscape photography that "like pornography, attempts to seduce the beholder by presenting an image divorced from its actual physical context." This photography cheats reality through the use of both special filters and its focus on atypical, monumental land forms separated from the surrounding landscape. As a result, we glamorize "scenic" spots at the expense of care for more productive overgrown woods, mosquito-ridden swamps, and empty plains.

Raw Heads: Even when an observer of details avoids having a cooked head, being immature or having poor intuition can choke off crucial understanding of implications. Lacking certain educational or life experiences, an essayist can be insensitive to the importance of a given detail in art, fiction, case studies, historical events, business deals, personal relationships, anything in life. Immaturity can easily result in taking certain details for granted and dismissing others too quickly. Immaturity can also butcher curiosity, allow impatience to bruise the complexity of details, or loosen insecurity to kill unfamiliar details. Educators will seldom admit that maturity has so much to do with wiring the thinking process. Insight does not enter the brain on a disc; it comes from mental software already sensitive to special input.

Bad intuition or lack of imagination creates the same problem as immaturity. One of the most dangerous unwarranted assumptions educators can make is that logical thinking has nothing to do with these harder to define elements. While intuitive insights finally need to be tested and thought through logically, intuitive knowledge is based on a culmination of hundreds of past experiences that, when remembered correctly, help live-wire the brain to find clues to understanding the significance of the detail at hand. In his book *Creative Evolution,* Henri Bergson points out that intuition is a type of knowledge that is superior to either instinct or intellect when those elements are forced to work independently from each other.

Some thinkers mistake using intuition to search for clues with considering emotional reactions to something in deciding its worth. Judging the worth of a creative work by its emotional results — whether it scares your pants off, jerks all the tears out of your eyes, chokes you on your own guilt, or makes you feel full of virtue in the face of evil personified — is called the *affective fallacy.* This judgment is a fallacy because a film, book, or painting might appeal to one's emotions but present a simple-minded view of reality in order to evoke those emotions. The worth of some works are decided by their ability to dramatize social, moral, and psychological insights — such works might arouse our emotions too, but their worth is not based solely on this arousal. Thin-minded writers, directors, and artists appeal to our emotions in order to give us the sensation that we have experienced something important, but in truth the details of their works do not describe reality, nor do they offer a new insight into reality. When people only care about entertaining or massaging their emotions, they run the risk of being made to care about unimportant, unrealistic, or undeserving positions.

Perceiving and articulating the ways people massage their emotions and mistake simple-mindedness for intuition can lead to helpful inductive essays. For instance, people often want to excuse bad behavior by claiming that they can intuit an inner goodness in a person who has otherwise run amuck. In "What You See Is the Real You" from *The New York Times*, Willard Gaylin, a Columbia University professor of psychology, argues that implications of actions reveal who people really are, not the feelings and intentions that lay dormant in their inner selves that are never realized. He asks, "Does it matter if Hitler's heart was in the right place?" He points out that the unconscious life of a man may be an "adjunct to understanding him" but not a substitute for his behavior in describing him. "The inner man is a fantasy. . . . It has no standing in the real world which we share with each other."

Aberrations of intuition aside, a strong thinker knows that intuitive feelings, unlike unwarranted assumptions, can short-cut longer thinking processes to find clues that still need to be tested. Intuitive minds can peel to the truth faster than minds dependent on step-by-step reasoning which slosh through reality and are then easily mud-eyed by quick or subtle changes. Intuition allows thinkers to fast reverse and fast forward to look for clues, using those clues as temporary reference points, exploring new sequences that might reveal a previous detail's missing implications. Sometimes this cross-word puzzling is called *lateral thinking* because the thinker is not *vertical thinking*, which would mean using details and implications as building blocks that must follow each other in a predictable, sequential order such as going from small ideas to the large ones they support. Successful business men, critics, parents, ministers, students, scientists, and others rely on strong intuition.

FALLACIES

Critical thinking and writing teachers often give students a list of labels that refer to ways the human mind intentionally or unintentionally cheat-jumps the gap between a detail and its worth. These are referred to as logical fallacies, but we think "fallacies that pretend to be logical" more accurately describes these blips in critical thinking. Going through the list of labels can numb the sharpest minds, so we have scattered the fallacies throughout this book, putting them in a context where a writer would be most vulnerable to a specific fallacy. You have already encountered a few above. Careful inductive thinking based on sound exemplification — using a number of examples, using detailed examples, and using the most representative examples — chokes out most fallacies.

If you want to review and sharpen your knowledge of all the fallacies in this book before an important debate, here is where they all are: *euphemism* (entire Scrub under Style unit), *equivocation* and *begging the question* (War Paint under Scrub in the Style unit), *ad ignoratum, shifting the burden of proof* (Introduction to this unit), *red herring* (Introduction to Peel under this unit), *misapplied generalization* and *affective fallacy* (Eclipse in this section), *intentional fallacy* (Deduction under Press in this unit), *tu quo que* or well poisoning (Synthesized Research under Press in this unit), *amoebas* (Splitting the Second under Time Warp in the Form unit), *empty abstraction* and *irrelevant appeals* (Introduction to Encircling in the Form unit), *false analogy* (Talking Words under Encircling in the Form unit), *fallacy of composition* (Sliced Pie under Encircling in the Form unit), *post hoc* (Flashback under Time Warp in the Form unit), *either-or fallacy, false dilemma* and *Ego Es Ibi* (Thirteen Ways under Layering in the Form unit), *ad hominem* and *ad misercordium* (Introduction to Uncorking in the Form unit), *Bandwagon* ("Are You Talking to Me?" under Uncorking in the Form unit). To see all these at their cheating best as part of a legal-drama, see Sidney Lumet's 1957 film *12 Angry Men*, a great depiction of a logical-fallacy pressure cooker.

WORKOUT: Write about anything that seems so unique, so ambiguous, so complicated, or so seemingly simple that your reader is either easily confused or takes the item for granted: a short story, a famous painting, an economic policy, an historical event, a building, a collection of sociological case studies. You should write about something you can observe directly, not through others: an actual document or report; a painting even if photo-copied; photographs, charts, blueprints; descriptions of events rather than editorials; interviews, a short story or poem. If you are writing in a classroom situation, the topic may depend on your instructor's ability to define the kinds of details that are important for observing that subject. For instance, analyzing a fiction writer requires careful study of that writer's organization, style, dialogue, setting, use of character; a painting requires observation of the title, colors, textures, composition, lighting, shape, as well as details of subject; an historical event means looking into documents, letters, eyewitness accounts, memoirs of participants. All of these are called *primary sources*. For now avoid *secondary sources*, which are analytical evaluations of the primary sources by other writers.

Begin by writing notes listing all relevant, important details, and then opposite each one, jot down your thoughts about each detail's implications or significance. These notes will take hours of time. Only after you have considered each detail on its own, should you begin to inductively form a general conclusion about the truth of its presence, meaning, or worth. This general truth will be your paper's thesis. What you conclude may be complicated or simple, but you must feel that it is something that surrounds and takes into account all the smaller implications listed in your notes. You can start or end your paper with your thesis, although most college professors require the thesis to be stated first. The whole paper must be devoted to describing and explaining how all your details and their implications support that thesis. Your paper will be much more complete and effective if you consider this a rough draft and subject it to requirements listed under "Press" and "Peel" below. For Samples, see the listing at the end of the unit.

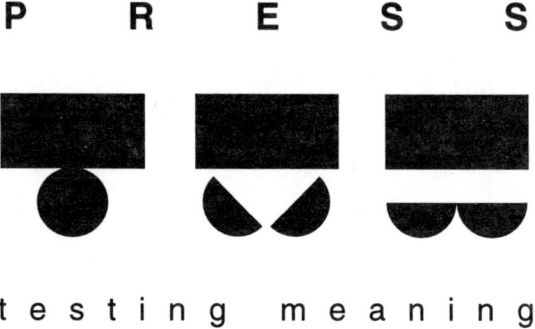

testing meaning

Aside from having details suggest their own implications, meaning can also be squeezed from details by pressing them against an outside standard of measurement. Whether writers argue or claim what something is; whether something is the same, not the same, better, or worse than something else; whether something causes something else, or whether or not something should be implemented, writers can supplement their inductive thinking through any combination of Deduction, Comparison and Contrast, and Synthesized Research .

DEDUCTION

Deduction in a logic textbook is explained with a series of circles crossing one another to demonstrate the problems that can occur when creating syllogisms, the bringing together of two statements to prove a conclusion. As a writer, the most important aspect of deductive thinking is that the thinker starts with a thesis instead of discovering one. This out-in-the-open, previously decided upon thesis or controlling concept is called a *hypothesis* or *major premise*. Before analyzing the subject matter for an essay, the writer puts on this hypothesis like a pair of sun glasses, screening in only those details with implications that support the hypothesis. Deductive reasoning is useful in deciding the extent to which a work of art conforms to a preexisting aesthetic philosophy; a diplomatic decision contributes to an historical movement; a business deal conforms to a past business practice or success; a personal relationship matches a psychological concept for a healthy relationship; a political event confirms a political theory; a legal precedent supports a legal case. In other words, deduction is thinking about how anything harmonizes with a preconceived definition or concept. Unlike a cooked head, the deductive thinker considers the hypothesis to be a tentative, vulnerable, start-up truth, accepting the concept with academic, rather than a personal, commitment. This allows the writer to melt the hypothesis away if it cannot be supported or proves to be unhelpful in understanding the subject matter being analyzed.

Very often an established hypothesis has matured through others' inductive thinking. In other words, a past thinker harvested implications of details and gradually discovered the hypothesis that the present essayist is now using as a start-up truth. However, the start-up truth is always vulnerable because it may not smoothly or realistically fit the present essayist's situation. The essayist might need to mill material to conform to the hypothesis, sapping the essay's credibility. Furthermore, there is never a guarantee that the hypothesis did carefully evolve in the past through inductive thinking or if it did, maybe the details that were used to inductively nourish this past hypothesis have changed. Also, when writers analyze someone else's work, they often try to certify their hypothesis by using the creator's intentions as a hypothesis. What people intend and what they finally create — a business proposal, a work of art, a legal case, a relationship, anything— are often two different things. Final creations are the yield of intentions but also of intuition, unconscious reactions, accidents that are capitalized upon, accidents that are not capitalized upon, and misunderstandings. This means that anything to be analyzed has its own life, essence, worth, or truth and its creator is always left behind. To judge the worth of anything solely by someone's intentions is called the *intentional fallacy*.

A more helpful deductive press is usually a philosophical stance. For instance, an essayist could start with an hypothesis established by feminists and use it to evaluate Shakespeare, or one by a scholar of nineteenth-century English romantic poets to evaluate a popular ecology-themed movie, the surrealistic painters' manifesto to evaluate a greeting card, a presidential economic policy to evaluate a bill passed by Congress, a work by Emanuel Kant to evaluate a Protestant moral stance, a conclusion made by any essayist in a college anthology to evaluate another writer in the anthology. In each case, the first work provides the start-up truth which screens in the details and implications from the second work which support that truth. Since other details and implications that do not harmonize with the hypothesis are left out, deductive thinking does not nurture original thought as much as it encourages interesting, often very helpful, connections with preexisting ideas.

A great short deductive essay is "Baseball Smadhi: A Meditation of the National Ritual" by Peter Gardella, first published in *Touchstone*, the Manhattanville College daily newspaper, later discovered by *Harper's Magazine*. The essay uses a mandala, "a design that aids meditation by drawing attention from its borders toward its center" as a hypothesis for understanding the game of baseball. Every aspect of the game is analyzed in terms of the mandala, including the pitcher's mound, "marking the center of a square," to returning home as completing the "cycle of life," to Jungian associations of three, to Martin Buber's definition of religious ritual being outside of time since "whether ten minutes or half an hour has passed has no more relevance to a baseball game than to a Mass."

Sometimes in working deductively, essayists consciously, or even intuitively, decide to have deduction give way to a more democratic Press. This happens when the writer decides to not only analyze all the details and implications from the primary source being analyzed, but unpeels and scrutinizes all the details and implications from the outside source which before provided only the hypothesis to judge that primary source. As this begins to happen, the outside source that provided the start-up truth no longer enjoys its major-hypothesis monarchy. At this point, the writer has moved from a Deductive Press to a Comparison and Contrast Press.

COMPARE & CONTRAST

Having a good friend brings with it the following experience. The friend appeals to us because of a combination of strengths, maybe social and psychological, moral and ethical, physical and stylistic, verbal and athletic, or intellectual and emotional. As we get to know more about any of these qualities, we become more aware of the friend's strengths and weaknesses. However, nothing brings these attributes and weaknesses more quickly into sharp focus than comparing and contrasting them to similar ones in another person. When we do this, positive and negative attributes we took for granted in the first friend intensify for one of two reasons: either because they are confirmed as plausible by seeing them again in a second person, or because they are contradicted by what we see in the second person.

For instance, the first friend may seem appealing because he or she always offers unconditional support for whatever we do. We enjoy this and take it for granted that friendship requires this attribute. Later we meet a second friend who believes that friendship is not based on unconditional support, this friend also congratulating us for positive achievements, but also offering helpful criticism when we fall short of goals or grow weak taking certain stands. By comparing friends, even on only this single issue, a discussion takes place in our minds because the contrast calls into question the worth of unconditional support and, ultimately, the worth of both friendships.

For an essayist, these mental discussions can put back-bone strength into an essay. Compare & Contrast can flash brighten material within only a phrase in an essay or can vertebrae the entire length of the piece. It can press out meaning for rough drafts even if those comparisons and contrasts crumble away before the final piece. Compare & Contrast can press one architectural space against another to sharpen what makes one an extraordinary problem solver, press two business deals against each other to account for the one with more promise, press two historical figures to confirm leadership qualities or fragilities, press two automobiles to close a more efficient purchase, press two political platforms to justify the more humanitarian position. When arguing, always anticipate details and implications your opposition will use against you and use these to Compare & Contrast with your details and implications. This Compare & Contrast will rebar your essay while crumbling the opposition's footing.

PRESS

A good collection of inductive essays that also uses Compare & Contrast is *For Keeps*, a collection of film criticism by Pauline Kael, who reviewed movies for over thirty years at *The New Yorker* and was the most influential American film critic of the twentieth century. Whether a movie was primarily an art or entertainment film, she was able to explore the implications of visual details, literary aspects, and historical precedents, all with equal care, using all the stylistic tools talked about in this book and often by comparing all the film elements to ones in other movies, paintings, and fictions. For many readers, Kael's essays became I-don't-agree-but-I-gained-helpful-insight experiences.

When unfamiliar details or realities are made clearer by comparing them to more familiar ones, such as comparing the details and functions of a medieval knight's horse to those of a business man's automobile, the comparison is called an *analogy*. In analogies, the emphasis is more on similarities than contrasts. See the Talking Words chapter in the Form unit for more on the function of analogies. On the micro-stylistic level, metaphors are implied analogies. Metaphors, where the word "like" or "as" is used, such as in "her lips are like roses," are called *similes* and are directly expressed mini-analogies.

In terms of explaining a very subtle, complex subject, one of the richest essays, employing equal amounts of Induction, Deduction, and Compare & Contrast in terms of a brilliant use of analogy has to be "Comics and Catastrophe," by Adam Gopnik in *The New Republic*. He carefully analyzes Art Spiegelman's cartoon-framed novel, *Maus*, a recounting by Spiegelman's father who survived the Holocaust. Gopnik skillfully dismisses those who see the comic book treatment as trivializing the event, and who want the Jewish holocaust to be depicted in an elevated style associated with religious art. He explains how Spiegelman turns the Jews into mice and Germans into cats in order to underscore how people can become as "helpless and doomed as mice fleeing cats — but they still think that they are people, with the normal human capacity for devising schemes and making bargains," and also in order to "give dignity to the sufferers without suggesting that their suffering had any 'meaning' in a sense that in some way ennobled the sufferers" Gopnik clarifies the issue with a telling analogy to a 13th-century Ashkenazi Jewish cartoon called the Bird's Head Haggadah, an image of a Passover subject too holy to be depicted realistically, therefore rendered in cartoon style with bird-headed worshipers; just as Spiegelman has a subject too horrible to be depicted, so he uses cartoon style to describe "the ultimate profanity, that must somehow be shown without being shown."

SYNTHESIZED RESEARCH

Often material for Deduction and Compare & Contrast must be researched, but research involves its own Press. Research has to do with looking up outside material and bringing it to bare on the subject at hand. Most people enjoy doing research "papers" in their heads, almost without knowing they are doing it. A person has a house plant and cannot decide where she should put it to get enough light. This person calls the nursery where she bought it, talks to a friend who has a similar plant, and maybe consults one or two books. All the advice from these sources blend or *synthesize* in the person's brain, resulting in a decision as to where to put the plant. After watching how well the plant does in this new place, these observations are meshed with the previous research about the plant to decide on an even better choice of location. The person has created a research project without knowing it. An even less conscious research project happens when a teenager makes a careful decision about dating a person, research consisting of several live interviews and phone calls plus careful "field" observations. Of course, as is the danger with any carefully done research, intelligent, synthesized material can always be scorched by one's emotions. Often the wrong person is dated.

In the academic world, the library is the primary research source. However, be forewarned — enter library waters only after mental conditioning. Whether researching a new refrigerator, tracking critics on a famous painting, or running down economic reports to confirm a business proposal, first analyze and inductively evaluate all the details of your old refrigerator, the painting, or the business proposal before wading into other material. As mentioned above, the actual items you are investigating are called *primary material*. After inductive analysis, the information from your researched or *secondary material* will mean much more because now your mind can Compare & Contrast all the details and ideas you have thought about and written notes about with the new material you are looking up. Your inductive understanding will help you to *evaluate* what you research: It will force you to ask whether the researched information adds to, complicates, or distracts from what you already think and whether the information is stronger or weaker than what you are beginning to believe. Without this ability to assess, your mind can get lost in a sea of material where every current and wave begins to look the same.

An essayist's researched, synthesized material can be used many ways. It can be used solely as introductory material that the primary experience is measured against deductively. It can provide Compare & Contrast material to be used throughout the essay to confirm or to argue against the essayist's inductively arrived at opinions. Often English instructors require students to use researched matter as their only material to inductively reach a decision, deleting any of their own analysis or inductive evaluation of the primary material. However, never rely on secondary sources simply because they are written by authorities. There are many writers with credentials who are poor writers, lack insight, and most importantly, do not develop their arguments carefully. When you simply use their name and credentials to validate an idea, you are committing a persuasion cheat called an *appeal to authority*. Always read critically, making sure other writers have inductively arrived at their opinions by using strong exemplification connected to implications with clear explanations. If they do not, even if their opinions agree with yours, reject their work and find stronger writers. On the other hand, do not ignore well argued points by writers you usually disagree with or you risk committing the fallacy of *tu quo que* , or well poisoning, dismissing insightful arguments because of others prejudiced, self-interested, or negative motivations. Learn from these arguments or carefully argue against them.

When taking notes from research sources, which might include books, internet information, television documentaries, interviews, and periodicals, put each idea on a note card rather than on a page of notebook paper. Putting each idea or details on its own separate card frees you to psychologically shatter that source into information bits which can be more easily rearranged, then shuffled together and synthesized for your own purposes. Also this allows the researcher to separate material from the source's style since so many outside sources, although knowledgeable, are not stylistically well written or have used organizational forms that are not compatible with yours. Keep a list, called a *bibliography or works cited* list, of all your sources with each one numbered or coded. Each note card should have only one idea in your own words, unless you want to quote it, and the code or number from your work cited list to remind you which source the material is from without writing that bibliographic information on every card.

Also on each card include the page number from the source because you will need it to make parenthetical references later. Most students think that parenthetical references and footnotes are used only with word for word, direct quotes from the source, but only the quotation marks (" ") signal that. If you use any ideas or details from a secondary source, you must give that writer immediate credit in your paper by mentioning his or her name and and page number. In academic papers, footnotes are for giving credit to another person's idea, regardless of whether it enters your essay in quotes or in your own words. Failing to give credit to another, called *plagiarism*, is tantamount to stealing. The final list of sources that you use from your bibliography in your essay is arranged in alphabetical order, author's last name first, entitled *Works Cited*, and is put at the end of your essay. There are many good research how-to books that have proper footnote and work cited formats.

WORKOUT: In order to make the paper you wrote under the Peel section richer, subject it to one or more of the three Press tests outlined above. Our favorite Press test is the Compare & Contrast check: one economic policy pressed against another one, a short story by one author pressed next to another one with the same themes by another author or even by the same author, one church's architecture compared to another's, one clothing store lined up next to another, a political argument pressed against another one on the same issue, two painters with different styles framed next to another painting on the same subject .

Compare & Contrast will help to underline certain details and ideas you have already noticed; other times it will force you to consider details you previously took for granted. In some cases, there will be so many important comparisons and contrasts that you will need to change your thesis. Include all these in your notes. Where you think it is helpful for the reader, include these comparisons and contrasts in your final paper. Never simply point out a comparison or contrast; always answer this crucial question for the reader: How does this difference result in a difference in implications? In other words, what difference does each difference make? The answers spawned here can become an essay's primary food source.

Next consider looking into secondary sources. What other writers have written about the item you have analyzed? This kind of Press can result in several kinds of discoveries. First of all, the opinions may refute your thesis. If so, you need to reexamine your implications. If you still feel your analysis is more correct, then you will need to synthesize any opinions arguing against you and with your own support, argue against these, showing how they fail to consider important details, implications, or lines of reasoning that you have found. On the other hand, some of your research will likely support your thesis. You will use these writers and their details, implications, explanations to support your thesis. An even more likely third thing could happen, and it could be from a source that agrees with you or disagrees with you, one that is poorly argued or well argued. Any source could give you information or point out details that you were not aware of beforehand and which you can now consider for use in your own argument.

While doing your research, you will see that writers mention definitions or theories. These can be used as major premises for a Deduction test. Depending on your subject, definitions and theories may be references to artistic and intellectual movements or general theories of economics, psychology, philosophy, literature, and politics, or legal precedents, moral values, and religious ethics. You may want to investigate these definitions or theories further, taking notes on many of their characteristics, and then explain how the item you have analyzed inductively under Peel above meets or does not meet those characteristics. This will allow you to show the reader either how typical or unique your item is compared to the expectations of those theories and definitions.

F I L T E R

expressing meaning

Whether doing Synthesized Research, Compare & Contrast, or Inductive and Deductive thinking, the essayist's final concern is to use style to connect details to their implications. Making the connection between a detail and its implication must be carefully modulated. It takes finesse. Sometimes the connection is forceful and clear cut; other times it is subtle. Creating this connective membrane involves either choosing the right verbs that directly connect details with meaning, using metaphor explained in the Fusion section under Style unit, or making use of the other techniques discussed under Style having to do with Flow and Pause.

DIRECT CONNECTION

An appropriate verb cleanly and directly grafts details to ideas or implications. The essayist first must decide how definitively or vigorously the two should fuse. For instance, sometimes details *strongly suggest* ideas: rain <u>symbolizes</u> growth; a crown of thorns <u>alludes</u> to Jesus; a long sentence describing the actions of an automobile or rattlesnake <u>represents</u> their movements; colors <u>signify</u> emotions, spiritual importance, or moods; a hedge of plants <u>exhibits</u> order and control. Other times details *reinforce* ideas that have been established earlier in the essay: light entering a chapel or window in a painting <u>emphasizes</u> the motif of unexpected hope; an unselfish action <u>validates</u> a person's love for someone else; metal furniture <u>underscores</u> the utilitarian mood of a room; the use of a specific word <u>sharpens</u> a writer's sarcastic perspective on a political situation.

Sometimes a detail can only *subtly suggest* an idea: dark clouds <u>hint</u> at worse times to come; a legal precedent <u>implies</u> that a law should be overturned; a low dining room ceiling *suggests* the protection of a primitive cave. Other times details *dramatically create* ideas: her decision to throw out the textbook <u>propagates</u> several creative thoughts about who she is; in a painting, the yellow sparkles of paint on the nude's body <u>unseals</u> her innocence; the husband's rejection of his wife <u>reveals</u> his cynical view of love. Still other times details define the limits of implications: the architect's use of hard edges <u>restricts</u> the occupant's awareness of nature as being chaotic, while the use of a long, wide windows opens the occupants to the vastness of nature; a B flat in a particular tune <u>confines</u> one's joy; the business's bottom line <u>focuses</u> on efficiency.

In every case, the verb helps connect the details on the left side of the sentence with the implications, suggestions, or meanings on the right side of the sentence. Use your thesaurus to find the verb that mostly accurately captures the strength of the connection between every detail and its meaning. If you have a difficult time finding connective verbal tissue, it may be because you have not first carefully, inductively thought out the most important implications of the detail.

METAPHORIC CONNECTION

Review the Fusion section under the Style unit. Since metaphors always carry a compressed load of associations, they effectively suggest the worth of any details onto which they are fused. For instance, in an essay about cement sculpture-furniture, art critic Peter Schjeldahl first made a list of details about concrete: it spreads quickly and then stops all of a sudden; it can conform to any mold but the mold must be tight, made with laborious care; it is not as supple and flexible as wood, clay, even plastic once it firms; it is impossible to change its form once it has hardened. In order to discuss the implications of these details, in this case to suggest that concrete is idiosyncratic, uniquely feisty, and taken for granted, Schjeldahl fuses all the physical attributes of concrete to metaphors. In his essay, he uses Line-Up and Break-Up metaphors, picking ones that are   associated with animate objects, a metaphor usually called *personification.*

For instance, Schjeldahl writes "Promiscuous, doing what anyone wants if the person is strong enough to hold it, concrete is the slut, gigolo of materials." Later he writes "Once it has set, what a difference! Concrete becomes adamant, fanatical, a Puritan, a rock, Robespierre. It declares like no other material the inevitability, the immortality — the divinity — of the shape it comprises, be the shape a glopped heap on the ground or a concert hall, ridiculous or sublime." The personified Line-Ups such as "promiscuous," "adamant," "fanatical;" the possessive Break-Ups taken from parts of prostitution such as "slut, gigolo of materials;" the metaphorical analogies such as "a Puritan, a rock, Robespierre," the Break-Up verb "declares," all connect concrete's physical attributes to an implied idea of concrete's worth. The metaphors give concrete a specific, unique presence that can no longer be taken for granted, a presence that is more active than the reader could have imagined. By capturing this active presence, metaphor establishes the implied thesis of the essay. Using some of those metaphors, a direct expression of the thesis might read, "Concrete has a fanatical, promiscuous soul, but a soul of a 'pitiless idiot' that 'will never notice' a viewer's derision."

STRUCTURAL CONNECTION

Aside from being an economical way of tightening material discussed in the Flow and Pause sections under Style, the actual structure of a sentence — both its word order and its use of punctuation — has the magical capacity to suggest how the details in a sentence should be perceived by the reader and then indirectly suggest what the details in a sentence mean. A sentence's structure echoes the reader's silent voice, inflecting the words to give meaning just as we give meaning to words with oral inflection when we speak them. Structure tells us how to read a sentence: which details to flow together; which material to give pause and stress. Structure is voice.

FILTER

As discussed under Pause in the Style unit, the Very Short Sentence can suggest many meanings depending on its context, including creating crankiness (as in the Didion example), anticipation (as in the Angell examples), or sarcasm (as in the Williams example). Long, flowing sentences have even more potential to create meaning. Consider again some of the sentences used as Samples in the Flow section of the Style unit such as Norman Mailer's sentence from *Of a Fire on the Moon* in the Freighting Samples. The structure of the paragraph-long sentence which includes so many details, tells us that the details have the importance of variables in an algebraic equation, whereby a change in one detail affects every other one discussed in the sentence. For instance, the fact that the craft is "going from weightlessness to one-sixth gravity" is effected by every other detail given in surrounding phrases, such as being "flown for the first time in the rapidly changing field of gravity of the moon" and "one-sixth gravity had never been experienced before in anything but the crudest simulations," and these elements are in turn hinged onto and altered by all other phrases in the sentence such as "the weight of the vehicle reducing drastically as the fuel was consumed" which implies that there is an interplay between the changing field of gravity and weight as fuel is consumed. Therefore, the writer does not need to overtly state that each detail is dependent on every other one: the flow of all the Lem details in one sentence declares that all are dependent on one another.

Packaging these information loads into shorter sentences would suggest a different meaning because each load would be disconnected by the reader's voice, requiring the reader to perceive the elements as independent from each other: "It was the first time the lem had been flown in the rapidly changing field of gravity of the moon. Of course, one-sixth gravity had never been experienced before in anything be the crudest simulations. Now the astronauts would experience going from weightlessness to one-sixth gravity. The actual weight of the lem would continue to be effected by how much fuel was consumed and that in turn would change the effect of gravity on the lem."

The different uses of length and structure to connote meaning are endless. So much always relies on what subject or content enters the structure. For instance, the following image from Flannery O'Conner's story *Greenleaf* of the "steady rhythmic chewing" Mrs. May hears in her sleep of a bull outside her bedroom, that "like some patient god" has "come down to woo her," is filtered through a sentence that uses length, exaggerated with catch-the-breath compounding, in order to suggest Mrs. May's breathless obsession, paranoia, desperation, and sexual yearning:

"She had been aware that whatever it was had been eating as long as she had had the place and had eaten everything from the beginning of her fence line up to the house and now was eating the house and calmly with the same steady rhythm would continue through the house, eating her and the boys, and then on, eating everything but the Greenleaf's, on and on, eating everything until nothing was left but the Greenleaf's on a little island all their own in the middle of what had been her place."

For a completely different purpose, Jamaica Kincaid, in "On Seeing England for the First Time", uses length to run together diverse motifs from English novels that she was forced to choke down while growing up as an Afro-American girl in Caribbean Antiqua. By running diverse motifs together, not allowing them the importance of their own sentence, Kincaid reduces each one to an inconsequential tick on a list, creating a sarcastic flow that hisses at the superficiality of the details she describes: "And having troubling thoughts at twilight, a good time to have troubling thoughts, apparently; and servants who stole and left in the middle of a crisis, who were born with a limp or some other kind of deformity, not nourished properly in their mother's womb (the last part I figured out for myself; the point was, oh to have an untrustworthy servant); and wonderful cobbled streets onto which solid front doors opened; and people whose eyes were blue and who had fair skins and who smelled only of lavender, or sometimes sweet pea or primrose."

FILTER 119

One final point about style, both in terms of structure and word choice. The microcosm of style is a rich topic for an inductive analysis in itself. For example, "Long Sentence" by Michael Kinsley in *The New Republic* is a two page inductive analysis of every topic, word, and grammatical choice in one crucial, long sentence made by 1996 presidential hopeful Reverend Pat Robertson, defending himself against accusations of being anti-Semitic. In part of the sentence, Robertson says we must ensure that the trend is "not for the elimination of the Jews." Responding to Robertson's call for caution through a style that combines a negative "not" with a horrifying situation, Kinsley replies, "Does Robertson think that anti-Semitism consists of wishing for the 'elimination' of the Jews? This is setting the bar awfully high."

Inductive analysis of written Forms, such as those discussed in the next unit, are also intriguing. Poetry includes an array of language forms and *Poetic Meter and Poetic Form* by Paul Fussel, Jr. remains one of the best books to clearly explain the implications of different metrical variations and stanzaic forms. For example, Fussell explains how the sonnet form allows a writer to exploit the principle of imbalance: the Petrarchan sonnet forces the poet to combine sexual build up and release with a rhyming pattern and length that allows a "relatively expansive and formal meditative process," whereas the twelve-line problem development and two line solution couplet of the Shakespearean sonnet invites "images of balloons and pins," a form that encourages "wit, paradox, or even a quick shaft of sophistry, logical cleverness, or outright comedy."

WORKOUT: Now that you have written your Inductive Analysis and have worked in crucial material from your Press tests, you need to smooth all your connections between details and implications by filtering them through all three methods discussed above. First, go through the paper with the Direct Connection in mind; then start over from the beginning with the Metaphor Connection in mind; then finally the Structure Connection. Often we tell our students that all these connections should be used to make the descriptions "sound like" the subject matter and make the ideas "sound like" the writer's attitude towards the subject matter. In other words, the style's tone should affirm your perspective on your subject matter. Your style is a metaphor for your perception of details and ideas.

F O R M

TIME WARP   LAYERING

ENCIRCLING   **3**   UNCORKING

REMAKING HUMPTY-DUMPTY

Aside from knowing how to craft with style and crack with thought, a writer needs to design a larger form to interweave a piece's ideas and implications. Typically this form might be a legal brief, a magazine article, a cookbook chapter, a business report, a history term paper. There are many alternatives to designing within any of these contexts. Sometimes style helps influence the shape of this form; sometimes the form decides the style.

Most English teachers have dictated what this form should be, reducing it to the following formula: Decide on a thesis statement. Start the paper off with that thesis statement and use the introductory paragraph to explain it. Cluster all similar details and their implications into three to five different paragraphs. Include enough explanation in each paragraph so that the reader understands how the details and implications in each paragraph support the thesis statement. Restate the thesis in a concluding paragraph.

This organization works because it is easy to follow and appears to be fail-safe. However, the precast bones of the essay's structure can protrude, distracting from the piece's meaningfulness. For instance, if the thesis is not first developed and tested as explained in the Thought unit, the format's argumentative structure dries out and turns insincere, or at best is a ghost of an outline. If the writer does not apply the stylistic choices discussed in the first part of this book, the material has no flesh, dehydrating the essay. Without critical thought and style, essays become tedious, unreadable exercises, but too often the form is an English-teacher-pleaser because over the decades teachers have made the essay's bone structure a holy relic that can do no wrong.

Strong writers never believe there is only one way to shape a large piece of writing, and hardly any of them base their essays on the academic thesis essay described above. Designing organizational architecture for any occasion can be creative and stimulating, often evolving from the function or purpose of the piece. Other times, past or prefabricated forms, including the academic essay described above, can offer a writer thinking-pattern clues, so that thought follows form for a while and then the writer adjusts the form so that it evolves into a unique variation of its prototype. The test of history is worth something. Whatever shape a piece takes, the notion that an ideal organization for writing exists is an illusion shattered by many learning-to-write books, beginning with the ancient Greek philosopher, Aristotle. His works on writing knocked the written world off the ancient wall; then he collected works back together again under new categories or modes, making various writing tactics easier for writers to perceive. He probably never intended those to be cast in bronze, and today he would create new ways for describing essays.

We have reexamined the forms of classic and contemporary essays, knocked them off the wall, and put them back together again, some as variations of classic forms, others as new forms, but not with the idea that any should ever be ossified in stone. We think Socrates would approve. Each form has its own pur-

FORM

pose, strengths, and weaknesses. All can be combined with each other to form countless others for endless applications, ranging from academic purposes to personal or practical ones. All should be strengthened with different degrees of elements described under the Thought unit, including Compare & Contrast, a Press device many English teachers have been trained to think of as an organizational form. All our designs are problem-solvers, forms effectively holding a mass of details and implications together in order to help the reader conceive new, truthful connections. Essayists typically shape in one of four ways: They narrate, define, divide, or disarm. We include discussion of the problems of each and possible design solutions under Time-Warping, Encircling, Layering, and Uncorking.

TIME WARPING

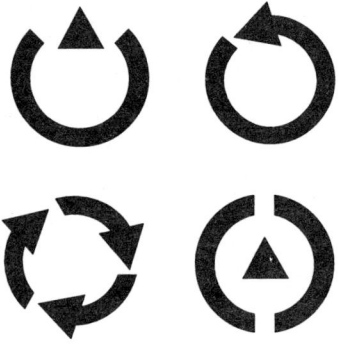

ways to narrate

Narrative essays, ones that describe a sequence of personal, scientific, business, political, or historical actions, pose interesting challenges for an essayist: In order to narrate, the essayist must story-tell, exaggerating some details to enhance, adding others to clarify, and editing out others to open the flow of the narration. In short, many of the best narratives blur the line between fact and fiction. The opposite can happen. Many works of fiction, such as Don Delillo's "Videotape," which is half-rooted in real events, blur the line between fiction and fact. Whatever the narrative piece, detailed organization of events in a time-frame clocks the reader's perception.

Time can be used and organized in countless ways, each method serving different purposes. Sometimes a writer may want to slow

TIME WARPING 125

down time, detailing an event that happens within a split second, as in Annie Dillard's "Total Eclipse." In his first book, *Writeful*, Gary developed a method called "Splitting the Second" to describe the capturing of this time, Glynis later broadening its application. Other times, the essayist may need to focus on poignant events that lead up to an important revelation or conclusion, leapfrogging through stepping-stones of time, intensifying the importance of each time-step by using present tense narration. We call this "Flashback." When each time-step is a revelation in itself, where time keeps resetting itself to create mini-climaxes, we see the piece as a "Strip Tease." Finally, "Raising the Dead," or having characters dialogue about events, allows for a blend of narration with debate that can transcend time. Essayists often combine two or more of these strategies.

The *point of view* from which the sequence is being told filters the narration. If the essayist wants to relate an event that happened personally while establishing an intimate connection with the reader, then the essayist often employs first person, or "I" point of view. However, sometimes the essayist may want to create distance from the narrated event, perhaps the tale being painful to relive or perhaps appearing too personally biased; then the essayist might present the events as if they happened to someone else, viewing them through the third person, "she," "he," "it," or "they" point of view. Maybe the essayist is writing about historical, scientific, or economic events; then the writer can create all-knowing objectivity by using a third person omniscient voice, which looks at life with a Cycloptic camera eye, spying on others' thoughts and capturing hidden details not possible from a fixed, real-life point of view.

SPLITTING THE SECOND

Writers must sometimes narrate brief, poignant moments of fleeting reality in which an event has lasting, significant meaning or which causes an important change in perspective. These fleeting moments present a challenging narrational task because, even though the action happens within seconds, the experience is so filled out with detail that it takes much longer to read and savor the experience than the actual event took in real time. In fact, the reader can only believe in the reality of the event if the writer makes it more vivid and detailed than it actually could be perceived in real time, where the speed of the event blurs many details. Therefore, the writer captures the action in slow motion, slicing the action into separate, smaller segments, "stopping the action down" like a physicist — whether the action is a passionate kiss, wolfing down a bowl of *chili verde*, the landing of a red-shafted flicker in a tree, or a single flight stage of a newly engineered space shuttle. Consider this excerpt from N. Scott Momady's *House Made of Dawn:*

"They were golden eagles, a male and a female, in their mating flight. They were cavorting, spinning and spiraling on the cold, clear columns of air and they were beautiful. They swooped and hovered, leaning on the air, and swung close together, feinting and screaming with delight. The female was full grown, and the span of her broad wings was greater than any man's height. There was a fine flourish to her motion; she was deceptively, incredibly fast, and her pivots and wheels were wide and full bloom. But her great weight was streamlined and perfectly controlled. She carried a rattlesnake; it hung shining from her feet, limp and curving out in the trail of her flight. Suddenly her wings and tail fanned, catching full on the wind, and for an instant she

TIME WARPING 127

was still, widespread and spectral in the blue, while her mate flared past and away, turning around in the distance to look for her. Then she began to beat upward at an angle from the rim until she was small in the sky, and she let go of the snake. It fell slowly, writhing and rolling, floating out like a bit of silver thread against the wide backdrop of the land. She held still above, buoyed up on the cold current, her crop and hackles were gleaming like copper in the sun. The male swerved and sailed. He was younger than she and a little more than half as large. He was quicker, tighter in his moves. He let the carrion drift by; then suddenly he gathered himself and stooped, sliding down in a blur of motion to the strike. He hit the snake on the head, with not the slightest deflection of his course or speed, cracking its long body like a whip. Then he rolled and swung upward in a great pendulum arc, riding out his momentum. At the top of his glide he let go of the snake in turn, but the female did not go for it. Instead she soared out over the plain, nearly out of sight like a mote receding into the haze of the far mountain. The male followed, and Abel watched them go, straining to see, saw them veer once, dip and disappear."

Instead of seeing the eagles' flight as a single general action — "Two eagles were flying and mating overhead"— Momaday breaks down each moment of action, harnessing subtle movements, carefully selecting details and using style to both fragment actions and flow them together. The general action "flying" is slow-motioned to see specific movements with specific verbs such as "cavorting," "spinning," "spiraling," "swerved," and "sailed." Strong writers know that every action is made up of smaller, related actions. For instance, if you were to follow a recipe which calls for a cup of chopped onion, you know you will be chopping; however, hidden beyond this seemingly simple task is a whole list of other actions: choosing an onion, purchasing it, taking it home, peeling it, and then chopping. The chopping aspect itself can be broken down further: the cook slashes the onion in one direction, slashes in another, and then slices the onion through both slashes to create small squares. Detailed verbs not only establish reality, they also create an overall mood or attitude. Without ever saying directly what the mood is, Momaday confirms that the experience was majestic or awesome. The verbs "cavorting" and "spinning" suggest agile playfulness, but also gracefulness, especially when looped with the speed suggested by the verbs "swerved" and "sailed." Aside from verb selection, Momaday carefully filters the scene by using color elements such as blue, silver, copper, clear, or golden, all gleaming visuals that suggest an ethereal tone as opposed to lime-green, rust, and purple — all colors which would plummet the mood earthbound. The subject of flight may seem to automatically create a mood of majesty or awesomeness, but no subject is an automatic pilot. Contrast Momaday's piece with Annie Dillard's splitting the second in "Stunt Pilot":

"Pitching snow filled all the windows, and shapes of dark rock. I had no notion which way was up. Everything was black or gray or white except the fatal crevasses; everything made noise and shook. I felt my face smashed sideways and saw rushing abstractions of snow in the windshield. Patches of cloud obscured the snow fleetingly. We straightened out, turned and dashed at the mountainside for another pass, which was made, apparently, on our ear, and fell away. If a commercial plane's black box, such as the FAA painstakingly recovers from crash sites, could store videotapes as well as pilots' last words, some videotapes would look like this: a mountainside coming up at the windows from all directions, ice and snow and rock filling the screen up close and screaming by . . . I saw the windshield fill with red rock. The mountain looked infernal, a dreary and sheer plane of lifeless rock. It was red and sharp; its gritty blades cut through the clouds at random. The mountain was quiet. It was in shade. Careening, we made sideways passes at these brittle peaks too steep for snow. Their rock was full of iron, somebody shouted at me then or later; the iron had rusted, so they were red. Later, when I was back on the ground, I recalled that, from a distance, the two jagged peaks called the Twin Sisters looked translucent against the sky; they were sharp, tapered. and fragile as arrowheads . . . I caught a snake in the salt chuck; the snake, eighteen inches long, was swimming in the green shallows."

In this flight, danger replaces grace. Dillard's verbs are much more unsettling — "smashed," "dashed," "shouted" — and even the fact that she uses many verbs which end in an edgy, quickly-spoken "-ed," as opposed to a rolling and lilting "-ing," adds to the tension. Dillard continues to make her flight rocky by using pausing, disconcerting, short sentences which force the prose to engine-stall. Dillard also filters the flight with mood-suggesting colors — black, gray, white, and red — serious colors associated with danger or oblivion.

Aside from verbs and colors, metaphors and other sensory details fuse reality with mood in both pieces. For instance, both attach selected details to snakes that make them different metaphors. Momaday's snake flickers "like a silver thread," becoming a symbol of the sun, and is a shared object of play which unites the male and female in a mating dance, whereas Dillard's snake "in the green shadows" is unexpected, an ominous reminder of life on the ground. Dillard fuses other details with metaphors which suggest earthy vulnerability: "fatal crevices," "the mountain looked infernal," "fragile as arrowheads."

Dillard slows the action through diversions, subconscious meanderings, such as dwelling on a video-action black box which the reader associates with plane crashes. This object would mental-sputter anyone flying with a stunt pilot. Dillard also includes other sensory details, not just what she sees, but kinesthetic details that register panic, "I forced myself to hold my heavy head up against the G's, and to raise my eyelids, heavy as barbells," and nerve-rattling acoustic details, "everything made noise and shook" and "somebody shouted at me." In contrast, Momaday's silence buoys the eagles' majestic flight.

In both pieces, details filtered through style prove reality. Strong writers know they must show, not tell. If Momaday merely told the reader that the mating flight was awesome, or Dillard told the reader that the stunt flight was nerve fraying, then only our faith would wing reality. Reality based on faith is always suspect.

ADIOS, STRUNK & WHITE

When a writer's style filters details so that they bond cohesively, the details prove a point of view or mood without the writer even having to tell what it is.

For different Splitting-the-Second tastes, read almost any great fiction. For instance John Hawkes, in *Death, Sleep & The Traveler*, splits dream-sequence seconds in order to satirize Freudian clichés about dream symbols. Also many memoirs contain poignant Splitting-the-Seconds, such as *Red Azalea* by Anchee Min, which splits moments of a betrayal Min was forced to take part in when she was the leader of the Little Red Guards during the Chinese Cultural Revolution. Some Splits capture almost non-existent moments. An example is Gretel Ehrich's *The Solace of Open Spaces*, where rich metaphors capture both the physical and mental movements of "smooth-skulled" winter.

WORKOUT: Gary thought of this assignment on a warm spring day, and Glynis expanded on it while watching a cooking show on television. Pick out a walking course that can be traveled within ten to twenty seconds, or focus on a simple meal which would take only a few minutes to eat. Both these events would normally occur too quickly for anyone to notice their small details and subtle changes. Put the walk or meal in slow motion by breaking it into at least three smaller time slots.

Force yourself to spend an hour taking notes. Look closely at small details, taking notes on everything: stains, light reflections, insects, aromas, textures, and colors. To help you notice all the sensory details, head two or three sheets of paper with each of the five senses. During the note-taking phase, stay away from qualifying or judgmental terms or abstractions such as beautiful, ugly, dirty. Write down only the details that make you think about these terms.

When you have three pages of notes, pick one of the following five moods: paranoia, ecstasy, surreal, amusement, serenity. This mood is your thesis or controlling idea and will help you to decide which details to include and which to omit. Without ever

TIME WARPING 131

saying what your mood is, organize your draft, describing the details in a way that suggests your mood. Use Break-Up and Line-Up metaphors to help create a second-splitting, mood-evoking description. Since you are describing a physical experience, telescoping sentences may be especially helpful. Flow and Pause can help underscore mood: Lots of flow can be calming and circular; lots of pause can help create tension. Realities made of details speak more powerfully than abstract or judgmental statements. Avoid the phrases "the way," "kind of," and "sort of" because they sound as if they mean something but say nothing at all, gobbling up chunks of space needed to use exact words to express a complex thought or observation. We call these phrases Amoebas. Filter them out.

COOL DOWN: Although this assignment will help build writing control and make interesting essays, Splitting the Second can also appear as a part of other larger pieces. Many times it is necessary to include a descriptive tract within larger narrations or arguments. In his "Critical Writing About the Visual Arts" course, Gary has tested students' understanding of specific artists by requiring them to analyze that artist's visual style and imagery and then invent a writing style which echoes that visual style. Instead of the moods listed above, students then use that style to describe the walk above and label the essay with the name of their chosen artist.

FLASHBACK

Replaying an experience that developed over time, finally resulting in an important revelation, can be enlivening and inspiring. Time needs to be rewound so that the reader first experiences the seeds of the unfolding event, participates in its development, and then gradually arrives at a final, substantiated understanding of that experience's importance. To reset the clock, the writer must first create a special time-traveled rough draft. This rough draft must be conceived backwards, starting with the conclusion, and then working backwards in time, traveling into an unformed past, the writer having no idea where he or she is going to end up in terms of the original seeds of the experience and its revelation. Flashback is an act of discovery back into time for the writer; then it is an act of discovery forward in time for the reader.

This is how the essay is designed. First the writer develops the conclusion: a carefully described summary or insight that is either personal, historical, scientific, economic — anything. This paragraph is placed at the end of the essay. Only after writing this conclusion to the paper does the writer then recall and describe the event that immediately preceded, defined, and assured the validity of the insight summarized in the conclusion. This second paragraph is a snapshot of the last crucial past situation which clenched the conclusion that has already been written. This second paragraph is then placed near the end of the essay just before the conclusion. Only after writing this second-to-last paragraph does the writer recall and discover a second situation or event, not one that supports the conclusion to the essay, but one that emotionally or intellectually carved the way

TIME WARPING

for the event captured in the second-to-last snapshot. This paragraph fills the third-from-the-last slot in the essay. We require our students to time-step back about four times from the conclusion.

Remember, these paragraphs are not necessarily examples in support of the conclusion; they are solely time stepping-stones that help the reader understand the next paragraph or slice of time that follows. The writer cannot always anticipate where hopscotching back into time will lead: The writer never knows which event to write next until asking, "I have just discovered and described event X, but what event happened before X that prepared the emotional, intellectual, or physical way for event X to happen before it occurred? Now I need to describe that event." When the essayist is finished, the reader will have the advantage of seeing the early seeds which sow each event, each one chronologically setting down roots for the next piece of growth.

Realize that you are not always looking for events that cause the next event, but ones that provide fertile ground for the next event. To suggest that one event creates the next one runs the danger of creating the *post hoc fallacy,* mistaking a causal link between two events simply because one quickly follows or precedes another. The reasons for certain actions are usually the result of a series of past decisions and reactions that come together in very complicated ways to create new actions and reactions, and these connections need to be carefully proved. The writer had to travel backwards in time first to create a voyage for the reader from the past to the present, which will result in a fuller understanding of that present, but not necessarily to prove that one event caused another event.

Flashback is a time warp that allows for the removal of chunks of time, speeding the reader forward to the next most important event. Because of these time-forward flashes, each paragraph must start with a time reference to help the reader know which time stepping-stone the essay has reached. George Kennan's essay referred to below uses phrases such as "Let us jump ahead now to the days, fifty-one years ago this past November," "Another change of scene," "Let us jump ahead again," "The scene shifts to Washington," and "Next picture" to open every paragraph or section of his essay. These transitions allow the writer to jump quickly to key events, leaving out anything that does not build towards the final revelation.

The next issue the writer must face is what tense to use to describe the past. Usually when we discuss something that happened in the past, we use the past tense: people in the past walked, talked, ate, loved, and fought. However, sometimes life's pulse becomes much stronger when past events are narrated as if they were happening in the present time. When a writer explores past events using the present tense, we join that writer in a very special reality where details seem both unreal, haunted by a backwards movement through time possible only in dreams and also super real, outlined with a clarity obtained only when considering events in retrospect. Therefore, instead of saying, "Ten years ago I walked into my lover's house; everyone was watching," the writer writes "It is ten years ago and I am walking into my lover's house; everyone is watching."

There are many good reasons for writing about the past in the present tense. When embarrassing or painful past events are in the past tense, the reader psychologically relaxes, knowing time has softened those events, but when an event takes place in the present, the reader is more alert, sensing that reality is still warm and can be modified. Delmore Schwartz's short story "In Dreams Begin Responsibility," from *The World is a Wedding* , is about a person dreaming that he is in a movie theater watching a movie about his parents courting each other in the past. Witnessing our parents before they are our parents has to be one of life's great embarrassments. Present tense Flashback brings alive that potent embarrassment that would usually be softened and faded away by past tense, such as finding out that the father is not yet sure that he loves the mother, the mother's father is not sure the father would make a good husband, the mother and father try extra hard to impress each other. Present-tense pain also stays

TIME WARPING 135

fresh in Alice Walker's "When the Other Dancer Is the Self," for *Ms. Magazine*, which jumps through crucial embarrassing childhood experiences that end with a dramatic acceptance and insight into a part of herself that the world could have found shameful. Present tense eliminates the secure feeling of retrospect, the superiority of being able to look back over time with distanced knowledge. Present tense allows the past moment to spit at the reader and writer.

George Kennan's article, actually titled "Flashback," for *The New Yorker*, flashbacks to his role as diplomat and American Ambassador to the Soviet Union, but first he explains why he uses the present tense to describe the past: "To stress the responsibility of these memories in speaking for themselves and to distance the young man who received the experiences from the elderly one who now recalls them" Kennan uses Flashback to underscore that we are two different, living, breathing people with different kinds of knowledge at two different times in our lives. However, Diana Hume George uses dramatic shifts between past and present tenses in "Wounded Chevy at Wounded Knee" to dramatize her growth from innocence when she married a native American carnie out of personal rebellion stemming from her romantic clichés about native Americans, to experience when she finds that he had always been a rapist; then describes a long present tense anecdote that exemplifies her understanding of the death of the Indian culture into which she married.

Some Flashbacks seethe. "On Seeing England for the First Time" by Jamaica Kincaid is a darkly hilarious Flashback that overwhelms the reader with the specifics of British culture that were crammed down Kincaid's throat, a black woman growing up in Antiqua. All of this is done in past tense, but the time zones overflow with Netting at its wicked best. *Betrayal*, a darkly humorous film scripted by the great modern playwright Harold Pinter, explores the cutthroat exchanges between two literary agents. The film is about the crucial stepping stones in an affair, but the sequence of its events is related backwards: We see the affair's last fizzles first and its hyperbolic jump-start last, a reversal of the Flashback strategy that sets up stunning ironies.

WORKOUT: To begin Flashback, craft your conclusion. Your conclusion is a description of yourself as a mature person, one whose previous naive view about something —religion, education, social respect, friendship — has been replaced by a more realistic, or more affirmative, or perhaps even a more cynical, position. Another option is to describe someone else's realization or a historical figure's revelation about an important issue. Assuming you are writing about yourself, avoid trite realizations such as "I no longer believe money grows on trees" or "It is very difficult to be a responsible adult." Limit this description to a specific philosophical concern rather than trying to describe your entire world-view. Formulating this section is the most difficult part of the essay, and even though it will come at the end of the essay, this conclusion will be fraught with the getting-started anxiety normally associated with composing an introduction.

Now work backwards. Once you have formed a solid conclusion, begin by going back in time to the next closest event which led to your revelation or conclusion. Describe it in detail, making sure you have given the reader enough details to understand how the incident could lead to the conclusion you have already written. Even though you are writing this section second, remember that it will not be the second section in you paper. It is the second-to-last section. To maintain intensity, keep all the verbs in the present tense. Once the second-to-the-last portion is completed, keep working backwards, asking yourself what experience must have prepared you or under-prepared you for the second-to-last event. This experience will form the third-to-last event. Keep working back, even if you end up in your childhood, until you have a chronology of events which lead up to your conclusion's present-day perspective. It may be that the body of your essay is spread over days, weeks, or years. Create too many events, and then cut back to the best ones so that you end up with about four or five incidents.

TIME WARPING

COOL DOWN: Rewrite your essay, making sure that all but parts of the conclusion are in the present tense. Make sure each section starts with a statement that lets the reader know what kind of time shift you are making. Transitions such as "The year is 1993 and I overhear my parents fighting" will provide order, while at the same time create a dream-like, time-warping, history-making sensation in which events appear to unfold moment by moment while the reader watches as if the event is happening for the first time. Play with order. Although your first draft simply unfolded events in the order they happened, it may be effective to switch around a few of those events in order to create drama, suspense, or add credibility to your essay. As always, should you accept this mission, revise with Flow, Pause, and Metaphor. Lastly, composing this essay is a difficult, emotionally-draining experience, but done earnestly, you will write a piece that shames the usual, boring, event-which-changed-your-life essay.

STRIP TEASE

As demonstrated above, Flashback depicts several seemingly insignificant events as they time-step toward one important revelation. However, other times, personal revelations, historical events, scientific discoveries, or economic developments are the result of several separate events, each one with their own climactic ending and sense of finality. In this unfolding of events, time seems to keep resetting itself, moves forward to a new ending, and then starts all over again. The sense of overall closure found in Flashback described above is absent. Instead, each section of the essay is a tease, pretending to be the last event and not clearly the part of a continuum. We call this narrative sequence Strip Tease. To capture it, the essayist must warp time to make the reader feel that the end of each mini-event is the end of the essay, only to be stunned by finding there is yet at least one more event or piece of information to unfold.

Aside from creating an element of suspense, slowly stripping off episodes with their own mini-climaxes allows the reader to savor each one, and also to perceive endeavors as never-ending since each unit of time is of equal importance to any overall conclusive ending. This essay works especially well when writing about a subject that in actuality has many interesting, unexpected twists and turns. However, an insightful writer can make the mundane or subtle exciting by both using style and by noticing crucial, subtle developments that most people take for granted within a small event. In this case, the essay becomes a macro Splitting the Second. Also, unlike with Flashback, each event that leads up to the final climactic event of the piece is described and evaluated in the past tense since the past tense helps to create a sense of finality, reinforcing the feeling that each part of the essay could be the finish of the entire piece.

A good example of Strip Tease was written by Marvin Kaye entitled "The Toy with One Moving Part," from *A Toy Is Born*, a collection of essays describing marketing success stories. In this piece, Kaye quickly lists what silly putty can do — stretch, shatter, pick up newsprint, mold, bounce — then dramatizes the sequences of accidents that shaped Silly Putty as a marketable product. Each event or accident is written about in enough details and mini-climaxes to make each a story in itself, each one allowing readers to feel that they are at the end of the essay only to be confronted by another twist of fate. In 1945, General Electric was experimenting with synthetic rubber for the war effort when an engineer happened to drop boric acid into a test tube with silicone oil. The glob bounced. Kaye declares, "Accident number one: Silly Putty is born."

With this miraculous birth of a new product, the essay seems to be at an end. Not so. Great products wither when they are are not marketed; so next comes "accident number two." This mini-

TIME WARPING 139

story picks up with the history of Peter Hodgson, a man who leaves home to sell everything from presidential candidates to tires, fails as a research consultant, watches his marriage collapse, is hired by a toy shop to publish a toy catalog, decides to include toys for grown ups, discovers a mystery goo circulating at cocktail parties, and puts it in the catalog. Kaye carefully describes and savors all these details. The chemical toy outsells virtually everything in the catalog. Again the essay seems to be at its end, but there is much more to come.

In fact, in the next section the chemical putty putters out. Once out of the catalog and onto the shelves, Hodgson finds that retail packaging cannot match catalog appeal. Sales tumble. Next comes "accident number three." Economically pinched, Hodgson is forced to put the putty in plastic "eggs," and they jump off the shelves; then orders mount from a few dozen each day to a gross a few weeks later and eventually five hundred a day. A writer for *The New Yorker* buys one for a friend, ends up writing about it, and sales bounce all over the place. End of story? Not quite. The Korean War erupts, there is a clamp down on defense materials, including some used for Silly Putty's guts. Hodgson is thrown out of business. Finished? Hodgson spends two years traveling after the war to reestablish Silly Putty. The end? No, kids start buying Silly Putty. It takes ten years to solve quality control problems for kids, such as detaching it from human hair and carpets. Finally, in the 1960's Silly Putty is a $6.3 million a year winner.

Strip Tease works especially well for tracking scientific discoveries such as "The Body in the Bog," by Geoffrey Bibby for *Horizon*, which starts, "My part in the story began on Monday, April 28, 1952, when I arrived at the Prehistoric Museum of Aarhus, in mid-Denmark, to find a dead body on the floor of my office." Bibby infuses the essay with mystery novel suspense to explain why a male body preserved in a peat bog over 1500 years ago was murdered, each developed source adding one more suspenseful puzzle piece to complete the mystery: a forensic specialist figures death to be from a throat slit; botanists study grain pollens to determine how the burial took place; archaeologists of Danish prehistory clarify A.D. 310 religious beliefs on afterlife; the Roman historian Tacitus describes a mother earth goddess that demanded human sacrifice around A.D. 98.; food studies reveal stomach grains that place the murder in spring. Explanations of each finding seem to be the last one, but there is always one more.

Helen Caldicott's essay "What You Must Know about Radiation" from *Redbook*, uses Super-literalism and irony to strip away the terrors of nuclear technology, starting with a story on uranium mining, inhaling radon gas, and the cancer that results fifteen to thirty years later, climaxed further by descriptions of what happens when infected cells go berserk, producing trillions of daughter cells instead of the normal two, expanding on this danger by describing uranium tailings, how they dominate certain landscapes simply by being wind borne. Just when the reader comes to terms with this he gets the 99 percent waste that comes from uranium; Isotope Unranium-28; melt downs; radio-active coolants; Stontium-90; and cancer-causing Plutonium, toxic for half a million years, one speck for every human lung on earth, being enough to kill all of us, are all described in bone-chilling detail. Enough? Caldicott still has more to go.

"A Worm from My Notebook" is a typical chapter from Richard Selzer's *Taking the World in for Repairs.* This piece starts with a wish that students of writing "eschew all great and noble concepts . . . matters that affect society as a whole" and instead seek out the exceptional, such as the drama here from the world of parasitology having to do with *Dracunculus medinensis*, the Guinea worm. While herding his cattle in Zaire, Ibrahim drinks water infested with microscopic crustacean Cyclops which are the "parent, pantry, and taxi" of *dracunculus*, which eventually cast off the Cyclops. This part of the cycle is developed into a Strip Tease that is peeled away for several more climactic shocks: inside Ibrahim's body the worm grows two feet; Ibrahim feels its body ridge his abdomen; finally *dracunculus* migrates to Ibrahim's foot, senses water, and breaks through the skin.

TIME WARPING 141

Ibrahim's several-days-long remedy twists the worm out. But this is not the end.

Economic events and geographical descriptions make for insightful Strip Teases. In *Paper Money,* Adam Smith explains the Great Inflation in Germany in the 1920's in a doomsday Strip Tease, moving from a description of pre-World War I Germany as a prosperous country with a gold-backed currency and expanding industry, to abandoning the currency in favor of borrowing instead of saving, to finance World War I, to growing inflation, to the shattering of confidence for law-abiding citizens, to conspiratorial theories and lack of faith in values of decency, to a social climate for Hitler to finally exploit. "The City by the Sea," by Shiva Naipaul from *Beyond the Dragon's Mouth: Stories and Pieces,* is a Strip Teased description of Bombay India. The theme of this piece is that "Bombay deceives at every level," an ideal thesis for Strip Tease. Naipaul shock-cuts the whole essay right from the beginning where an unexpected international tennis tournament ends, "the spell is broken," and an unseen, dwarfish, "less-than-human crew" owns the courts with their brooms. The essay moves from nightmarish evening life to a glitzy film industry; from wealth to opium dens; from tuberculosis to plans for a New Bombay on neighboring islands; from mass migration of people to mass migration of rats; to incredible lists of what people do for work, including cleaning ears of passer-bys. After each section, the reader is constantly left whispering, "You mean, there's is more?"

Almost all good fictions employ some strip tease, but "Will You Please Be Quiet, Please?" by Raymond Carver, later used as a basis for a vignette by Robert Altman in his film *Short Cuts,* is an especially dramatic example. In regards to moves put on his wife by another acquaintance at a party years ago, each of a husband's questionings is delivered with an it-was-a-long-time-ago, it's-all-right-to-talk-about-it-now nonchalance, so that in a how-did-we-ever-get-off-on-this-subject tone, the wife is to gradually reveal more and more about her sexual escapade. Each step seems like the last one: a kiss, a breast grope, and finally sexual intercourse. Even this is not the final strip: Now fuming, the husband must know if the acquaintance "came" in her.

WORK OUT: Review an important time in your own life that was made up of several mini-events — a family problem, an athletic or dramatic event you watched, a long school or work project or conflict, a legal problem — or research an important development in a writer's, politician's, or artist's career; an historical, scientific, or political development; a philosophical or religious movement. You need to center on at least four mini-events that have their own mini-climaxes, the last one representing a final major outcome of the whole development.

In order for each event to stand on its own, you need to take plenty of notes before you start writing. There are three kinds of notes to write down for each mini-event: details that you know are important at the time of the event; details that will only be important in retrospect, looking back at the event from the present; details that are not literally or directly important to the event, but symbolically foreshadow the final outcome of the piece, such as messages on posters or newspaper headlines, a line in an irrelevant letter or movie on television, background dialogue from a social group or from a song lyric.

As you write your notes into each paragraphed section of your essay, keep in mind that by the time you get to the end of that particular section, you want the reader to feel that so much has happened and has come to fruition or failure that there could be no more to read. The essay appears to be finished after each section. This tease can be accomplished in two ways. At the end of each section, stress those details that create calm, quiet, utter failure, ecstatic success, satisfaction; then at the beginning of the new section, use transitions that call attention to the abruptness of the next event such as "Accident number three," "It was not over," "The nightmare started again," "That was only the beginning."

Because of the suspense Strip Tease provides an essay, by the end of it your reader will have paid strict attention to each development and having intensely followed each developing sequence will find the conclusion credible, no matter how incredible it would have seemed by itself.

RAISING THE DEAD

Pretending that different points of time from the past can merge with one another in one moment of time has several advantages for the essayist. Imagine dialoguing with the past, or bringing past thinkers into the present moment to test their philosophical, economic, scientific, or theological theories on our world. Time travel and created characters are the elements of fiction, but when these characters narrate what they have witnessed and discuss its significance, fictional techniques can enliven nonfiction debates.

One of the most informative time-mix narrative debates in writing happens in Fyodor Dostoyevsky's "The Grand Inquisitor," a chapter from his famous Russian novel *The Brothers Karamazov*. Ivan tells his brother Alyosha about imagining Jesus returning centuries after his death to Spain during the Church's inquisition to rid the country of heretics, but when Jesus reappears, he is thrown into jail by the Grand Inquisitor. Most of the chapter is a philosophical dialogue in which the Inquisitor talks to Jesus, narrating his view of the world's general response to Jesus, and trying to justify his rationale for arresting Him. In essence, Dostoevsky uses the incident and dialogue to pit "the exceptional, vague and enigmatic" that the Inquisitor says Jesus represents against "miracles, mystery, and authority" that the Church champions. The debate: Which makes humans happier? The argument is lengthy and carefully developed, but creating this mini-narrative drama and having Jesus Himself listen at a time when the Church was at one of its most powerful and violent moments, gives the argument both everyday-life and cosmic potency. Steve Allen brought a more playful tone to this time travel strategy with a television panel made up of famous guests from different time periods meeting on a panel to discuss a large range of philosophical issues.

Another method of mixing time travel is for the writer to take part in the past by imagining being there. In an issue of *American Heritage* magazine, the editors put together an essay titled "I Wish I'd Been There," a compilation of entries by such great writers and scholars as Stephen Jay Gould, Noel Perrin, Annie Dillard, Alfred Kazin, John Kenneth Galbraith, and others. Each writer was asked to narrate one scene or incident in American history that he or she would have liked to witness by "being a fly on the wall." By placing their psyches back in time, imagining being in the midst of a past event, the writers unlocked historical details that revived its original breath, something almost impossible to do when looking at an event as an outsider from a temporal distance.

For instance, historian Walter Lord finds the Golden Spike ceremony at Promontory Point, Utah, on May 10, 1869 to celebrate the first time the nation is linked coast to coast with a railway, a moment so full of promise that he chooses returning to it as a panacea to the darkness of modern day realities. Like a primitive tribesman entering the phantom world by putting on a spirit mask, Lord steps into A. J. Russell's famous photograph of the celebration and begins to decipher the unknown details of the scene: "I want to mix with that boisterous crowd of track layers, soldiers, dishwashers, gamblers, and strumpets. I want to listen to the 21st Infantry band thumping away. I want to watch the cowcatchers touch. I want to sample the bottle of champagne held out by the man standing on the Central Pacific's locomotive Jupiter. I want to know who the lady is in the exact center of the preliminary photograph, but who vanishes in the final, climactic shot. I want to know the identity of the one man in the picture who turned his back to the camera. Was he just inattentive, or was his likeness perhaps posted as 'WANTED' in every post office in the West? I want to watch Leland Stanford swing his hammer — and miss the golden spike." If history books raised the dead like all the entries in this essay do, no one would ever wonder what the past has to do with the present, inflate the past into enshrined monuments, or need to memorize events for history tests.

Another taste of this approach was "A New Year's Meal of Their Dreams" by Laurie Ochoa and Ruth Reichl in *The Los Angeles Times* , a stew of responses by Los Angeles's most well-known chefs who were asked to describe the New Year's meal of their dreams. Some thought of meals from their past, some thought of famous people who cooked well, such as Thomas Jefferson and Archestratus, others thought of locales, or some when the first meals from foreign countries entered the United States. The articles's total impact recreated the complex dimensions of food culture and history.

There is one more version of Raising the Dead which does not necessarily have to do with time travel, but it does have to do with using fictional or real characters to narrate incidents and breathe life into an argument that might expire if written in straight prose. The ancient Greek philosopher Plato's *The Republic* is one of the earliest examples. Plato develops all his arguments by having his friend and teacher, Socrates, present allegorical stories and arguments to an agreeable student who responds positively to Socrates's probing questions. For instance, in the section known as "The Allegory of the Cave," a short narration about men who see shadows instead of reality and are threatened by anyone who has, Socrates adds that "in the world of knowledge the idea of good appears last of all, and is seen only with an effort." The pupil cordially struggles through with, "I agree ... as far as I am able to understand you." This response adds little to the argument, but it is enough of a response to remind us that there is a thinking, feeling person behind the ideas, and that we are in the company of others who are grappling with understanding those ideas. Dialogue dissolves book pages that otherwise could trap and mummify ideas.

This same spirit Raises the Dead in the witty dialogue of James Boswell's biography *The Life of Samuel Johnson*. Johnson is the eighteenth-century moralist reported on by his much younger, best friend, Boswell, who primarily dramatizes the dialogue between the two. Boswell sets items up for argument by dragging Johnson on an arduous journey in the Hebrides, arranging for him to dine with notorious, unlikable people, and then asking Johnson a range of questions having to do with the sacred and the profane. Boswell: "I asked him what he thought was best to teach children first." Johnson: "Sir, it is no matter what you teach them first, any more than what leg you shall put into your breeches first. Sir, you may stand disputing which is best to put in first, but in the mean time your breech is bare. Sir, while you are considering which of two things you should teach your child first, another boy has learnt them both." You will find more modern witty-dialogue-as-philosophical-track in . . . *And Then I Told the President: The Secret Papers of Art Buchwald* by Buchwald, a compilation of his syndicated columns, essays almost always done as make-believe dialogues that are disguised, satiric comments on everything from politics to fashions to psychological mentalities. Chit-chatters include correspondents hiding out from Presidents in gym lockers, opposing political figures trapped together in a rescue boat, children using school prayer to do better on the school tests, a husband and wife having an affair with each other only to return home to boring selves, and Pilgrims who decide growing beautiful lawns is more important than growing produce.

In the same spirit as Buckwald's characters, cartoon characters by artists such as Linda Barry, Matt Groenig, Charles Schulz, and Garry Trudeau are actually two dimensional dialogue prompts before they are visual entities. At their very best, even the characters' settings are visual killers, focusing steady attention on philosophical discourse: there is very little movement of body positions between frames, little dramatic lighting, and virtually no shifts in perspectives common to super-hero and romance

TIME WARPING 147

comic strips. Even more powerful is Art Spiegelman's *Maus*, a novel written in comic book form narrating Spiegelman's conversation with his father, a Nazi holocaust survivor, who in turn narrates his experiences living in German-occupied Poland. Unusual distancing is created by turning the participants into animal people to underscore philosophical arguments. See the reference to Adam Gopnik's essay on *Maus* listed in the Thought section.

WORKOUT: Have someone from the past reappear and confront someone in the present. The possibilities are endless: A present day rock singer discussing music with a classical composer; Einstein correcting a present day scientist's use of physics; a talk show host refereeing a panel of philosophers from different time periods; a well known writer asking for advice from Shakespeare; a historian getting spit at by an ancient king. Use the event to define, evaluate, or propose ideas. Keep past personalities in character by researching and being clear on their perspective about related issues. Also, if you can study anything they wrote, analyze their writing style and imitate it for their dialogue style. Almost ten years ago when Glynis enrolled in Gary's "Humor in Literature" course, she wrote a paper that discussed important attitudes that shape male and female relationships by having Dr. Ruth, who hosted a popular television show giving frank sexual advice, argue with the Wife of Bath, a passionate, scheming life-force from Geoffrey Chaucer's medieval *Canterbury Tales.*

Another way to Raise the Dead is to find a manuscript, letter, painting, dialogue, photograph, or story and imagine yourself taking part in it as another character. Use this opportunity to imagine details that help give the reader a clearer idea of what was being argued or depicted in the work that would normally not be thought about. You may need to research the context or setting of the work.

A third approach, discussed above, is to try reconstructing a dialogue between make-believe characters who argue a point. One way to do this is to imagine this dialogue taking place in fifty cartoon frames and then heightening each part by cropping the argument into chunks of four to five frame strips each, one published each day in a newspaper. If you have visual talent, you could draw the frames; otherwise, use stick figures. Use good writing style in the language balloons since your dialogue must be as rich and detailed as if you wrote it in a paper.

ENCIRCLING

ways to define

When several writers write about the same personal relationship, business deal, artistic experience, scientific development, or political decision, the writer who defines that phenomenon the most fully and clearly usually ends up replacing all the other writers' visions of reality. Strong definition forges belief. Weak writers short-circuit definition by using authority, faith, common sense, or moderation to substantiate their view of reality. Depending solely on these notions as an argument is called making an *irrelevant appeals* because any of these sources or notions are vulnerable. Although they deserve consideration, they all have inherent weaknesses: authority can be wrong, mired in self-serving values; faith can be unreliable, seduced by time worn fantasies; common sense can be simple-minded, ignorant of subtleties; moderation can be weak, restrained in emergencies and a killer of spontaneity. Thomas Jefferson would have snapped his crow quill if someone had suggested that the Declaration of Independence was an unsound document since it lacked what would have been considered a moderate stance at the time he wrote it.

Also, authority, faith, common sense, and moderation are not notions we know through our physical senses, but are intellectual conceptions or abstractions. Unless a writer establishes the worth, reality, or meaning of important abstract words, the writer's argument risks becoming unclear, misunderstood, or powerless. Without careful definition, those words become *empty abstractions*. To assume that abstract concepts mean the same to everyone seems logical, but it is a fallacy. For instance, if someone writes an essay on political action that tells people to do something with moderation, the essayist must first convince the reader what the word "moderation" means since different readers might have very different and limited understandings of that word. Most people would not have the emotional strength or moral certitude to meet Aristotle's definition of moderation. (See the Aristotle entry under Sliced Pie in the Layering section.)

Most teachers discuss definitions in terms of single words and in terms of denotation (dictionary meaning) and connotation (implied associations). Often teachers point out that an analogy or narration can help to define a word, and we have added some other ways to explore meaning in Talking Words. Strong writers also know that definition goes beyond defining words and includes defining sweeping events and obscure histories, undetected movements and omnipresent forces, complex problems and intricate solutions. Blood Flow and Animation offer strategies for encircling those realities. In addition to the strategies below, definition essays may include any of those strategies discussed under Layering, Time Warping, and even Uncorking.

TALKING WORDS

Usually abstract words such as "love," "purity," "coolness," "sensitivity," "spirit" become the most complex and important subjects for writers. Since these words are forever changing and their lives take on more and more implications, defining an abstract word can take part of an essay or suck up all the space of an entire essay. When it does, it is called a definition essay, one of Glynis' favorites because the definition leads to a philosophical digression. Words represent reality, and reality is always richer than it seems to be; so discussing an abstract word becomes an exploration into both ideas and language. There are different strategies for exploring an abstract word, each one providing one panel that hinges to the others, all ultimately shaping the meaning of a word. Strong writers use as many panels as they have space for to build a stronger defense of the word's worth.

Language Reference Resources: Language reference books might include a desk dictionary, especially the *Oxford English Dictionary* (OED), a thesaurus, a book of etymology, or a book of famous quotations. The dictionary gives the standard meaning of a word, a mere start to build on or work against since through usage in different contexts the implications of words outstrip dictionary meanings. The opposite direction, moving back in time, is also helpful. The dictionary strips words to their stems, revealing insight into the original meanings of a word that may have become too often taken for granted and then lost over time, changed through select usage. For instance, essayist Michael Ventura, in his essay "A Dance for Your Life in the Marriage Zone," after describing a fight with his wife, considers the word "forgive" by breaking the word into parts and studying the original meaning of each one:

Pause at the word: "for-give." "for-to-give." Forgiveness is such a gift that "give" lives in the word. Christianist tradition has tried to make it a meek and passive word, turn the other cheek. But the word contains the active word "give,' which reveals its truth: it involves the act of taking some thing of yours and handing to another, so that from now on it is theirs. Nothing passive about it. The differences in desk dictionary meanings between common stem words used for different parts of speech, such as the words "prude" (noun) and "prudent" (adjective), sometimes dust off new clues about origins and implications. However, the prize blood hound is the *Oxford English Dictionary* or OED. This multi-volume dictionary marks a word's inception and then continues to sniff out the history of each word's changing meanings over years or centuries. For instance, many Victorian writers in the nineteenth century used the word "disinterested" to mean objective, or without hidden agenda, as in "Pip was disinterested in his father's will." Today "disinterested" can imply bored or not interested, so if Holden Caulfield was disinterested in his father's will, then he would be thoroughly apathetic about its contents. In her essay on friendship titled "Noble Companions," Gail Godwin uses the OED to make an important point about the word "friend":

> I seek (and occasionally find) friends with whom it is possible to drag out all the old, outrageously *aspiring* costumes and and rehearse together for the Great Roles; persons whose qualities groom me and train me up for love. It is for these people that I reserve the glowing hours, too good not to share. It is the existence of these people that reminds me that the words "friend" and "free" grew out of each other. (OE freo, not in bondage, noble, glad; OE freo, to love; OE freond, friend).

By showing the linguistic or historic link between the words "free" and "friend," Godwin discovers a forgotten dimension of the word "friend" and can then build a special definition for the concept of friendship that lives in her relationships, but has been lost in the present usage of the word.

The thesaurus provides synonyms, each with a slight difference

ENCIRCLING 153

in meaning, any one of them capable of instantaneously expanding the word-web. Comparing and contrasting an abstract concept to its synonyms encircles the original word, then radiates its subtle nuances. Highlighting and pondering these distinctions yields good philosophical fodder. For instance, "Cowardice," a piece in *Sunrise with Seamonsters: Travels and Discoveries* by Paul Theroux, carefully explores the word "cowardice," comparing it to morality, fear, and other personal abstractions in order to create new sympathies for the word's concept. Sometimes synonyms come to light in unexpected places. William Least Heat Moon's *Blue Highways* is the account of the author's travels along the back roads of America. While driving the blue highways, Heat Moon considers the meaning of many words. Often, the strangers Heat Moon meets provide the writer with important word distinctions. After Heat Moon explains to one man, Cal, whom he meets in a roadside diner, that he was fired from his job, the stranger thesauruses Heat Moon:

> I notice that you use the work and job interchangeably. Oughten to do that. A job's what you force yourself to pay attention to for money. With work, you don't have to force yourself. There are a lot of jobs in this country, and that's good because they keep people occupied. That's why they're called 'occupations.

Not only does Cal make an interesting distinction between job and work, but he also brings in a new synonym, "occupation," for comparison and contrast. A thesaurus is like a case-load of Cals.

Books of famous quotations pop out word surprises the same way children's pop-up books turn the two dimensional world into three. Look up a word or, if the word is obscure, look up a synonym for the word, and instead of a flat definition, the word springs alive in the meaningful context of a well thought out quotation. That quote is usually famous because the quoter noticed an unusual, ironic, or intelligent aspect of the word and carefully articulated its meaning in a well crafted sentence. To define the word, quote the quote and discuss its meaning. Also consider how the word comes up in old sayings, nursery rhymes, adages, clichés, lines from the dialogue of a movie, television shows, advertisements, and lines from songs: Does the word have the power to amuse, cruise, or fuse? Many famous quotes often come from literature — a novel, drama, poem, or film — and these quotes can help give an example of meaning. You can also use quotes from less literary sources--an advertisement jingle, a public sign or billboard, or even a bit from a stand up comedian. Be sure to always cite where you received the example and give the writer credit.

Abuse Excuse: Another way of defining a word is to say what it is not by showing how the word is abused or misused. For instance, cliché-bust by ruling out the usual, obvious definitions of the word. Following through with negation, or explaining what a word is not, immediately vaporizes preconceived notions of a word, clearing a path in the reader's head for a fresh look at a writer's definition. Gail Godwin cliché-busts in "Noble Companions," her essay defining "friends," in her introduction: "The dutiful first answer seems programmed into us by our meager expectations: 'A friend is one who will be there in times of trouble.' But I believe this is a skin-deep answer to describe skin-deep friends." By quickly ruling out the overused, there-for-us-when-we-need-them notion of friendship, Godwin opens her essay to previously unexplored possibilities of the nature of friendship.

In a doll-house-buster written for *Salmagundi,* essayist Daniel Harris begins "Cuteness" by proposing that images normally labeled as cute, such as stuffed animals and So Shy Sherry dolls, are actually closely related to the concept of the grotesque, where disturbing deformations actually create the disproportions we find so cuddly. The pitiable, helpless, stubby-bodied, swollen-armed dolls are seductive because they imply a helplessness that arouses our sympathies. Harris lets the definition creep out even further: We impose this notion of cuteness on children because our parental ego needs to perceive them as being more vulnerable and physically maimed than they really are. A corollary to Harris's essay is "On Ugliness as a Basic Injustice" by Francois Giroud and Bernard Henri Lévy in *Women and Men: A*

Philosophical Conversation, a dialogue between the co-founder of *L'Express* and the philosopher/ playwright. Their discussion defines the paradoxical qualities of ugliness, including its sexual seductiveness. For a definition to the flip side of ugliness, Nancy Huston's "Dealing with What's Dealt," in *Salmagundi*, explains the pain of "beauty," something she knows about as a woman who is a successful French writer and who is also beautiful. She carefully covers the positive and negative aspects of beauty and stress tests these by comparing French and American attitudes towards beauty. All these essays explain what a word is not and show how how it is abused or misused.

Stress Test: A completely different way to explore the meaning of a word is to subject it to different social pressures; then observe if the word performs differently. There are many social stresses that determine what gets squeezed out of a word: age, economics, ethnicity, education, geography, gender. Consider gender. Many abstract concepts have different connotations when applied to or used by either sex. If a writer were defining "sexy," the essayist would want to show any differences in how sexiness is defined by a woman versus a man. In her essay "Waiting," Irish writer Edna O'Brien claims that while women wait for love, men "wait for the promotion, they wait for the kill, they wait for the prize, and one has only to watch the antics in Parliament or in the Senate to see with what libido each is waiting for his moment to rise and strike a blow that will vanquish his opponent . . . . Men wait for women, too, once they have decided this one is the one, but they wait more busily and so little atoms of dread are likely to be diffused and tossed up and down so that they scatter."

Ethnic pressure is another stress test. In her essay "The Meaning of a Word," Gloria Naylor shows how the word "nigger" has many different meanings depending on the ethnicity of the person using the word. The same differences appear when testing a word by the generation using it. Words such as "peace" and "honor" meant very different things to the World War II generation compared to the Viet Nam War generation. Just when you cannot think of another social group with which to stress test, Vicki Hearne looks at the meaning of words from a dog-happy point of view, and by doing this in "What's Wrong with Animal Rights" for *Harper's Magazine*, she gives new meaning to definitions of "happiness" and "rights" while challenging our sentimental attitudes toward animals.

Exemplification: Both anecdotes and analogies can clarify the meaning of a word or concept. The *anecdote*, or short narrative, can be a truthful, experienced episode or an invented one, as long as it fuels real-life interest in the word. Another way to develop an original point about a word is by drawing an *analogy,* making a comparison between the abstraction and a specific situation which is less abstract, thereby making the abstraction more accessible by making it more concrete. When an analogy does not work to do this, but instead makes the abstraction unclear by not accurately paralleling the concept, it is called a *false analogy*. Strong analogies are extended similes that Press truth like Compare & Contrast (see the Press section of the Thought unit) to intensify elements that create similarities or subtle differences with the abstraction.

In "On Being Black," W.E.B. Du Bois, an intellectual and writer for the NAACP, skillfully uses anecdotes to define what it meant to be a African American in the early part of the twentieth century. For instance, in response to his "pale and positive" friend's remark that Du Bois is "too sensitive" to whites' reactions, Du Bois offers several horrific episodes that would make anyone cringe. Some are quickly mentioned in a list — "The milkman has neglected me. He pays little attention to colored districts . . . . The women in the streetcar withdraw their skirts or prefer to stand. The policeman is truculent . . . . My job is insecure because the white union wants it and does not want me," — while others are developed into complete anecdotes. For instance, Du Bois responds to his white, maybe fictional, friend's remark "I should think you would like to travel," with a page long narrative on what blackness means in terms of Jim Crow, black only, waiting rooms, and Jim Crow railroad cars. The narrative

ENCIRCLING 157

starts with details of how buying a ticket is even a torture, involving airless waiting rooms with horrible seating, waiting until tickets are sold at the other window to whites, the confusing and ignorant behavior of the agent who overcharges, and then the narrative details of the journey in the car where "the plush is caked with dirt," "impertinent white" newsboys hound people to buy "worthless, if not vulgar, books," conductors reserve information only for whites, and "As for toilet rooms — don't!"

A contrasting definition on being an African-American is offered in "On Being Black and Middle Class" by Shelby Steele. Like Du Bois, he offers personal anecdotes to clarify *both* "black" and "middle class," which in turn depend on his defining concepts of victimization and victim status. In order to explain these concepts, Steele discusses being in a "double-bind" — here this bind is the "trap" of being both black and middle class. In the beginning of his essay, to articulate his understanding, or "epiphany," that throughout his life he had been in a double bind and not realized it, he uses an analogy by comparing his awakening to another type of realization about a different kind of bind: "It was like the suddenly sharp vision one has at the end of a burdensome marriage when all the long-repressed incompatibilities come undeniably to light." By comparing the two double binds, Steele effectively draws in those readers who have no experience in being both black and middle class.

Netting: (Review Netting in the Flow section of the Style unit.) When asked what a word means, we usually have to choreograph a dance that encircles the word with a list of associations. What if someone asked, "What is spaghetti?" You would serve up a bland batch if you limited its reality by simply answering with the synonym "pasta." To serve up a fuller course, you would give ingredients — semolina flour, eggs, and and boiled water; you would list usages — sometimes served in Italian restaurants with sauces such as marinara, pesto, clam, garlic and olive oil; you would give out eating instructions — gets wrapped around your fork with the help of your spoon and generally one strand never quite makes it into your mouth, requiring slurping through pursed lips, like a fish sucking a worm; you would hint at what it tastes like — mild, smooth, slightly eggy. Flow techniques, such as Netting, can combine all of these associations to serve a seven course word meal with a surround sound of meaning. In characterizing Heathcliff in Emily Bronte's *Wuthering Heights*, literary critic Donald Stone, in *The Romantic Impulse in Victorian Fiction*, was unable to flesh out Heathcliff's essence in a simple word or phrase, so Stone resorted to a stream of terminology, gestalting a definition for the dark romantic hero of the novel: "Heathcliff in particular has been viewed as an anarchic force of nature, a mythic figure thrust into the real world, a Byronic-derived Satanic outcast, a Marxist proletarian-rebel, a representation of the Freudian Id, and a reflection of the heroine's adolescent narcissism." In fact, Netting can work for any of the strategies above: a whole paragraph which lists everything your term is not, a list of well arranged synonyms taken from a thesaurus, or a list of quotes and common usages of the word.

To see all the above strategies in action, do not exclude looking up the old masters, such as the great Renaissance writer Francis Bacon, whose "On Suspicion" explains the reactions of different groups to suspicion, such as disposing wise men to irresolution; explains what suspicion is not, something remedied by procuring to know more, and discusses the word as used under different circumstances. Or flip through *The Enlarged Devil's Dictionary* by Ambrose Bierce, the late nineteenth-century American writer, who cuts to the cynical aspects of definitions. Examples: "DICTIONARY, n. A malevolent literary device for cramping the growth of a language and making it hard and inelastic. The dictionary, however, is a most useful work." "HISTORY, n. An account mostly false, of events mostly unimportant, which are brought about by rulers mostly knaves, and soldiers mostly fools." "HAPPINESS, n. An agreeable sensation arising from contemplating the misery of another." Sometimes the best "dictionaries" are compilations of others ideas that cover all the approaches of Talking Words. "Time on his hands, love in his heart and Webster's Dictionary on his Mind" and a follow up essay, "On the scent of that most elusive of illusions — defining time one and for all ...," both by Jack Smith for the *Los Angeles Times*, point out the limitations of defining "time" and then compiles an array of imaginative definitions from readers and theologians defining "time" by using several of the devices discussed above.

WORKOUT: It is important to choose a word that has special significance in your life, a word that infuriates you, a word you have been victimized by, a taboo or dirty word, an abstract label that invites simplistic thinking such as "step-mother" or "hero," a word that is often misused, or overused such as "fantasy" or "hate." Subject your word to at least three of the Talking Word strategies; then begin to draft paragraphs with each one. After you have composed several rough paragraphs, begin to arrange them into the most effective order. For instance, often essayists will start with the language resource references as a way of opening up new possibilities for the word, but other times an anecdote creates more immediate interest in the word. You decide. For a final paragraph, Netting helps the reader to imagine the varied usages of the word spreading into the world; other times discussion of the word in a famous quote gives the word final stick. Strategies which define abstract terms can also be used as part of any careful argument or persuasive essay. Good writers know that an argument may be weakened or that their point of view is vulnerable to attack when abstract terms are not carefully defined.

BLOOD FLOW

Encircling a large reality that is more prevalent or omnipresent than the reader suspects presents its own defining problems. For instance, in his book *Memesis, the Representation of Reality in Western Literature,* Eric Auerbach explains that the Hebrew writers made God in the Old Testament more omnipresent than the Greek gods simply by never having God meet in council with other gods to reveal His motives; and by not letting the reader know where He has been between episodes; and by not giving God physical attributes, something Michelangelo did for every Sunday school student much later. By being nowhere in particular, God came to be everywhere.

More worldly omnipresent phenomena can be placed in time and space. A writer communicating the prevalence of something has the task of dramatizing its magnitude so that the reader obtains a realistic sense of how overwhelming or all-encompassing that reality actually has become. A strong writer knows that for most people these realities flow undetected, hidden below the skin of life's normal hustle and bustle. There are three techniques to describe and define this reality for the reader without mitigating its prevalence.

Fact Spraying: One essential technique is to bombard the reader with an endless, unrelenting stream of facts — dates, times, locations, numbers, people, foods, product names, parts, economic groups, professions, case studies, contexts — any details that will flow a consistent layer of reality over the piece of writing. For example, in her book *Distant Mirror: The Calamitous 14th Century,* historian Barbara Tuchman defines the overwhelming force of destruction created by the bubonic or black plague by

ENCIRCLING 161

racing us from one place to another, one time to another, one death count to another, so that we are forced to watch the disease reproduce and flow over the map of Europe. There is no pause; there are hardly any transitions. A typical entry mentions that "By January 1348 the plague penetrated France via Marseille, and North Africa via Tunis. Shipborne along coasts and navigable rivers, it spread westward from Marseille through the ports of Languedoc to Spain and northward up the Rhone to Avignon, where it arrived in March. . . . In Paris, where the plague lasted through 1349, the reported death rate was 800 a day, in Pisa 500, in Vienna 500-600. The total death in Paris numbered 50,000 or half the population." The map fills and over spills. Many essays that define the prevalence of a reality, shift from one spray of related items to another, each one forming a paragraph worth of material. For instance, in other parts of the essay, Tuchman shifts to sprays describing physical maladies or theological solutions. All of these topics define the magnitude of the disease.

Martian Point of View: Creating a knowledgeable person, or imagining what such a person would think about a specific omnipresent reality, gives a writer two advantages. The persona's shock about what should be prevalent and what actually is, allows the writer to discuss the omnipresence of one and imply the other. John Gliedman and William Roth use this Martian point of view in their book, *The Unexpected Minority,* which defines the permeating prejudice towards the handicapped. In this essay, the "Martian" is an imaginary person from an advanced industrial society who "genuinely respects the needs and humanity of handicapped people." This person is constantly put in situations where expectations are not met, thereby dramatizing the prevalence of a disappointing or unbelievable reality.

For instance, Gliedman's and Roth's persona would "take for granted that a market of millions of children and tens of millions of adults would not be ignored," and so would expect to find cheap automobiles that could be driven by paraplegics, simple gadgets for domestic use, researching of prosthetic devices with the same enthusiasm poured into space industry research. He would expect to see disabled people in books, television shows, cartoons, advertisements, factories, resorts, political action committees, and in school rooms in the role of teacher or principal. He does not. The reader then is forced to view and concede to wide-ranging evidence that what should be true everywhere is not true anywhere.

Foiling: Aside from lists, the reader becomes more aware of the scope of a given reality when constantly reminded of unusual details, ones that crack the complacency of a reader who beforehand felt comfortable believing that reality was narrower in scope. Narrowness supports normalcy; the unusual prepares the reader for expansion of vision. For example, aside from fact spraying to dramatize the worldly predominance of the plague, Tuchman shows how widely and consistently the world goes awry, how wherever the black plague touches, our normal expectations are also blackened. She shows how the actual symptoms of the plague seem unnatural, removed from the realm of normal pestilences: "everything that issued from the body — breath, sweat, blood from the buboes and lungs, bloody urine, and blood-blackened excrement — smelled foul." Such abnormalities creep in throughout the entire chapter, including leaving bodies of relatives outside for dogs to drag away, allowing women to give last rites as priests quickly die off, children and parents abandoning each other, and villagers dancing in merriment hoping their own absurd reaction will fight off the absurd disease. All these details serve as a foil to the normal expectations we have of disease, break those expectations, and tooth-pick our eyes for a wider ranging horror than we normally expect.

Gliedman and Roth provide foil against the normal by demonstrating how able-bodied people's minds perversely twist when confronted with the disabled world. For example, when normal people notice someone else limping in the distance, they immediately gut-wrench, feeling "pity, revulsion, or an interest in the unusual" but, as the limping person draws closer, revealing only

ENCIRCLING 163

a temporary cast, they feel a sense of relief. The mind of a normal eye-sighted human creature makes other fantastic, irrational assumptions when viewing an older male with an eye patch, immediately assuming this to be a person with a dark past and "a capability for just enough brutality to add a trace of virile unpredictability," but viewing a seven-year-old girl with one evokes fear and pity. Famous disabled people — Franklin Roosevelt, John Kennedy, Elizabeth Barrett Browning, Alexander the Great, Beethoven, Edison, Freud — are not thought of as people who succeeded despite their handicap, but people who overcame it, as if it was not an essential part of who they were. By constantly demonstrating how we have pinched ideas about the disabled, the writers help us understand that "to grow up handicapped in America is to grow up in a society that, because of its misreading of the significance of disability, is never entirely human in the way it treats the person within." Through our abnormal reactions, this idea is firmly established as a wider ranging reality than the reader could have ever imagined.

Defining natural cycles almost demands Blood Flow. "To the Potter's Field" by Edward Conlon is a stunning, almost mystical account in *The New Yorker* that spooks the reader with endless facts about the numbers of homeless people who are buried in New York each year, how their burials take place, the people who bury them, and where the homeless dead come from. A more refreshing mysticism is captured in *Pilgrim at Tinker Creek*, one of Annie Dillard's hypnotic and exhausting flashes of the surprising growth networks and miracles-made-from-the-taken-for-granted that occur in nature. Dillard's Blood Flow leaves the reader's mind buzzing. A colder Blood Flow on nature takes place in *The Formation of Vegetable Mold, Through the Action of Worms, with Observations on Their Habits* by Charles Darwin, the nineteenth century father of evolution, botanist, and geologist. Here he overwhelms the reader with the importance, prevalence, and magnitude of the work of earthworms.

Omnipresent subtleties need Blood Flow to sharpen their realities. Trickling flow streams are defined in "Rarity," a chapter in

The Size of Thoughts by Nicholson Baker, who proves how many rare things surround us that we are oblivious to. Baker does this by bombarding us with the details of model airplanes, the intricacies of movie projectors, the magic of reading aloud, the quirks of punctuation, the complexities of filthy slang, the mind as lumber. The entire world opens up as an unusual gift that is both scientific and metaphoric all at once. Even more subtle is an outline of the variety of sighs and reasons for them throughout the world by Bernard Cooper in "The Fine Art of Sighing" in *Paris Review* which describes various kinds of sighs throughout the world and the reasons for them, the scope taking the reader's breath away.

Some Blood Flows create nervousness and alarm. "Los Angeles Notebook" in *Slouching Towards Bethlehem* by Joan Didion is a Blood Flow of fire statistics, helter-skelter radio talks, scientific details on dry winds, and edgy street behavior that captures the transient soul of Los Angeles. "A Woman's Work" for *Harper's Magazine* by Louise Erdrich is a dense, metaphorical immersion into the trials and states of mind created by parenthood, especially motherhood: "It is uncomfortably close to self-erasure, and in the face of it, one's fat ambitions, desperation, private icons and urges fall away into a dreamlike *before* ." "Forgetting" in David Ehrenfeld's *Beginning Again: People and Nature in the New Millennium* is especially alarming, swamping the reader with frightening instances where we assume knowledge to be cumulative, but in fact "the more advances we make, the more we forget." He cites disappearing earthworm experts, the absence of anyone who knows "at what point in animal evolution was the porphyrin molecule (such as hemoglobin) first adopted for use specifically as an oxygen carrier," and graduate students who do not even know that comparative biochemistry classes once existed to teach such material.

Some Blood Flows are quick, sharp cracks such as "An Appeal to My Readers" from *The Green Book* published in *Harper's Magazine,* where author Crad Kilodney creates a hilarious attack on Perrin Beatty, Canada's print and film censor, by immersing

ENCIRCLING 165

the reader in a flood of clichés, exaggerated ways we have of saying how we want someone killed. At the other end of the emotional spectrum, "Patriotism Revisited" by David W. Powell, written for a creative writing class at the University of Arizona and reprinted in *Harper's Magazine*, conveys the utter horror of war. The grisliness of the Viet Nam War has been spilled before, but never so condensed and unrelenting as here, with entries running from "Discovered brain matter on barbed wire I was stretching out" to "Circled over El Toro air base for two hours so that President Johnson could land and be photographed greeting returning veterans."

WORKOUT: Write a Blood flow about an attitude or philosophy or condition that permeates a larger social strata, geographical area, or time span than most people realize. Topics might include attitudes about food, sex, chemical abuse, or health; perspectives shared by custodial staffs, teachers, advertisers; natural phenomena such as flies, earthquakes, oxygenators; abuses such as those perpetuated on waitresses, older people, and secretaries. Before you compose, make a big list from your observations and maybe do some library research to beef up your examples. You need to examine the unexpected nooks and cracks where no one usually looks. Use at least two of the devices listed above and the Flow techniques discussed in the Style unit. Blood Flow works by being unrelenting, with quick transitions, if any at all, and never slowing down for readers to catch their breadth.

ANIMATION

Science book and documentary film writers who define wild life and scientific events often clip the wings of their own fresh, nothing-taken-for-granted wonderment and excitement because they fear losing their "scientific objectivity." The epitome of this self-clip takes the form of blanched identification manuals, flooded reference books, and textbooks filled with drained prose. The psychological, if not overt, assumption made by these writers is that language is "objective" when it has the cliché terseness and flatness of mathematics, a debatable assumption in itself based on novice, cliché ideas about math in the first place. The other assumption is that all details, to be treated objectively, must be treated with equal importance, one blending into the other, as opposed to prioritizing or emphasizing important, defining details.

A case in point is Roger Peterson's bird-manual description from *A Field Guide to Birds:* He describes a bird that "runs on the ground (tracks show 2 toes forward, 2 aft.). Large, slender, streaked; with a long white-tipped tail,shaggy crest, strong legs. White crescent on open wing." (Song, 6-8 dovelike coo's descending in pitch . . .") The reader would have field trouble because so many of the bird's characteristics are shared with other birds, and Peterson avoids using style or organizational strategy to help the reader absorb the unique reality of this bird. Instead the reader's consciousness sinks into a swamp of information bits. There are three ways he could have made this bird fly: Using a riddle introduction, building problem-solution paragraphs, and using style metaphorically.

Riddle Introductions: Three things must be done to create a riddle introduction. First, the writer isolates the most dominant and

ENCIRCLING 167

unique details of the bird, putting aside detailed explanation of these as well as minor or less unusual details shared with other birds. Second, the dominant and unique details are presented in short, compound sentences (sentences that combine with a connecting word such as "and"), written usually from a third person point of view (he, she, it, they), sometimes in first person (I, we). This style creates a riddle-like rhythm that showcases crucial details without a lot of clutter. Third, the writer does not reveal the bird's name until the end of this introductory paragraph. By withholding the bird's name, the opening details attain a life of their own that presses firmly into the reader's mind, still uncluttered by the self-satisfaction of knowing this name without first having to pay close attention to details.

Another bird writer, George Hollister in *National Wildlife* magazine, opens his description of the same bird Peterson describes above with the following riddle introduction:
> "He's half tail and half feet. The rest of him is head and beak. When he runs, he moves on blurring wheels. He can turn on a dime and leave change. He doesn't need to fly becausehe can run faster. He kicks dirt in a snake's ace, and then eats the snake." What is it?

At the end (even though we might have guessed) we are told: A Roadrunner. If the reader goes no further, this introduction dramatizes the most crucial defining details needed to identify the bird. Imagine textbooks where all definitions of machines, body organs, historical figures, political structures, diseases, psychological disorders, scientific instruments, and other complicated objects or events, opened with a riddle introduction. We would remember more essential details. Consider student Alicia Eddy's riddle introduction for "The Kidneys" : "They take a lot of shit, but are tough regulators. They work for bananas to make you strong, but if treated badly, they can kill you." Riddles are memorable. If textbooks used this strategy, we could all pass biology tests without having to study.

Problem-Solution paragraphs: After the introduction, each remaining paragraph of the essay must organize material so that the reader is first involved in one, seemingly impossible problem that the bird— or as suggested above, historical figure, body organ, political structure, piece of technical equipment — must solve, and only then, in the second part of the paragraph, reveal how the entity being defined solves that problem. Too often writers do the opposite, immediately starting new paragraphs by telling the reader interesting or amazing abilities the animal has, such as bizarre mating maneuvers, impossible feeding habits, or genius engineering skill, before dramatizing, or even mentioning at all, the problem the animal overcomes by its unique ability. Likewise, writers explain how a political structure solves certain problems without entangling the reader in those problems first; they explain what equipment can do before overcoming the reader with the problems that need to be surmounted in the first place.

Day for Night, a film by Francois Truffaut, dramatizes the problem-solution nature of all creative endeavors. This feature film, though, is in essence a definition piece, demonstrating what a feature film is by dramatizing the problems that must be overcome to make a film. The film is composed of a series of logistical problems, mostly having to do with the actors' personal lives but including production problems and how each one is solved to finish the film. *Skyscraper* is a documentary film of the problem-solution nature of creative enterprises, a six-part PBS production that documents dozens of unimaginable designing, contracting, and constructing problems in building a New York skyscraper, each problem described in detail, leaving the viewer wondering how such a project could ever advance; then each one is expertly solved with architectural talent, diplomacy, and construction finesse.

Writers are probably not careful in developing paragraphs this way because they are no longer astonished by the problems they take for granted. Familiarity can mind-zap the most learned. If problem-solution strategy were consistently applied to everything we need to learn, we believe educational systems would become super-conductors. Does anyone really appreciate trigonometry, a wondrous mathematical invention, before being immersed in an engineering problem that requires it as a solution? Do young students really appreciate the United States's political structure based on a checks-and-balance systems unless they first view or read about the terror that exists when that system is absent? Does anyone remember how a general won a battle without first experiencing the pressure of that battle's initial importance and how deadly the obstacles looked before the battle? Too much of what we learn has to do with solutions, and their problems are either blitzed or ignored.

Hollister builds his problem-solution paragraphs by first describing, with threatening details, the roadrunner's hot environment and hyperactivity, both conditions which would seem to dehydrate the bird. Only when the reader's mouth dries, does Hollister mention the roadrunner's ability to locate shade and to feed on reptiles of high water content. Likewise, he dramatizes how difficult a long snake would be for a bird without teeth to digest before revealing the roadrunner's reliance on digestive juices to gradually burn the oversized food little by little. Other writers would simply rely on a checklist of easy solutions — the roadrunner eats animals of high water content to keep from dehydrating and uses its digestive juices to digest large snakes — assuming the reader will find these solutions fascinating. Permanent learning occurs when the mind solves a problem, not when it memorizes a solution.

Style: In Hollister's introductory riddle, he is not afraid to exaggerate with statements such as "half tail and half feet." Some writers would argue that this is not "objective," but seen in a flash, this is exactly what the roadrunner looks like. Fossilizing a roadrunner into "long white tail, shaggy crest," as Peterson does, makes the roadrunner unidentifiable and is perhaps a less accurate depiction of the overall visual image the bird presents. Later, in the body of the piece, Hollister also avoids bird manualrea by utilizing freighting sentences to realistically capture the smoothness and interrelated actions of roadrunner: "He dashes in circles around a coiled snake, stops within striking distance, shuffles his feet, swishes his tail in the dirt and stirs up a blinding cloud of dust."

The issue of inventive style over "objective" blandness to capture scientific reality is especially clear when comparing Norman Mailer's passages describing the Apollo landing on the moon in his book *Of a Fire on the Moon* to *Journey to Tranquility* by Hugo Young, Bryan Silcock, and Peter Dunn. Listening to the actual audio exchange between Control, Eagle, and Houston moments before landing on the moon, is exciting even without understanding the pelting, technical data the three are radioing to each other. The sentences are terse, with constant requests for readings on alarms. As soon as an outside writer decides to be helpful and comment on this exchange, interrupting its original tenseness with explanation, the original fire of the danger and excitement of the rapid fire urgency is threatened by the writer's neutering-needs to sound "objective." For instance, Young, Silcock, and Dunn write, "Apollo II was past the point any previous flight had reached, plunging into the most dangerous and unpredictable twelve minutes of the mission. Houston and Eagle exchanged terse, bullet-like packages of technical data as the seconds ticked away." These sentences do not create the urgent tone that made either the voyage or exchange sound as gut-wrenching as it really was. These writers tell the reader that the mission was dangerous rather than kiln-fire a description with a style that clear-glazes the event with danger and excitement.

Mailer uses Flow, Pause, and Fusion to blaze the voyage into a believable danger and real commitment:
> Boxed in their bulky pressure-suits, tied in and swaddled ike Eskimo children in baskets, all move bulky, always in fear of rapping a bank of switches with the insensitive surface of their suits — "You're so clumsy and there's so much force required to move inside the suit," Aldrin had said, "That everything is WHAM! I could bump right into you and maybe I wouldn't even know it"— constrained in vision, they began their powered descent. The motors of the descent stage were fired. Once again they braked. Once again the reduction of their speed

ENCIRCLING

began to bring them down from high velocity to low. Now they came below the orbital parameter of fifty thousand feet. They were committed. They would land, or they would crash, or they would abort and return to Columbia, but they could not try it again.

To believe that a bland style is an "objective" one is a subjective decision based on cultural assumptions that Mailer proves are not true.

WORKOUT: Combine your own experiences with internet and library research to build an Animation paper. Your purpose is to breathe life into a subject that has been suffocated in the name of "objectivity" by having a stale, encyclopedic, textbook treatment. Subjects could include animals, technical equipment, management or political systems, physiological parts, historical people or events, engineering projects, even an inventive person's biography. When you research material, realize that it will most often be written in a manner that does not take the Animation techniques above into account. Include any reading that does in your own paper and expand it, but be sure to give the source credit through proper work-cited documentation.

The principles of specificity and juxtaposition discussed under Netting in the Style unit are important to building your introduction, even though it will not not be shaped by long, flowing lists. To craft your introduction, make a list of the most unique and predominant details of the object you are describing, but do not include any details that are shared by too many others within the group to which your item belongs. For instance, if you are describing an engineering project, there would be nothing unique about mentioning that it took years to develop. What project does not? However, by being more specific — maybe the project took fifty years to develop — you will have a detail worth including in the introduction.

When you are ready to start composing the introduction, arrange the details into short compound sentences in first person or third person. The end result should create a riddle-like rhythm that helps show-case the most defining information: "He smells . . . but smells like . . . ." "He will always . . . but will never . . . ." "Sometimes he looks . . . and always looks . . . ." "He tolerates . . . however he enjoys . . . ." Notice that these sample compound sentence set-ups suggest interesting juxtapositions, such as paradoxes, ironies, seeing the same issue once from the subject's perspective and then once from the viewer's perspective. For instance, "He smells microscope size food, but you can smell him from fifty feet away." Remember, the purpose of the introduction is to load the most crucial material into a short amount of space, usually one third of a page double-spaced, typed, so that if the reader goes no further, he or she still takes away crucial, memorable information. Mention your subject only at the end of this introductory paragraph.

As you build the body of the paper, remember that most of your source material will make the mistake of taking problems and obstacles for granted and instead quickly give the reader material that is solution oriented. For other zoological or biological assignments, read "On Being the Right Size" in *Possible Worlds and Other Papers* by J.B.S. Haldane, a good background source for writers setting up problems that animals must overcome. This renowned authority on heredity outlines the way different sizes and shapes solve problems or create them for animals. For instance, a film of water on our bodies weighs a pound but means nothing; it adds up to a large enough burden on a mouse to sink it. Throw a mouse down a thousand yard mine shaft and it survives; a rat dies; we break; a horse "splashes."

For the body of your paper, often you will need to imagine the problem your subject must overcome, either by doing more research, by knowing the limitations of other related items, or by imagining the problems human beings would have trying to overcome a similar problem. What would it take for us to catch a hoofed animal that runs over fifty miles an hour or to filter microscopic impurities from liquid substance that had unusual properties? These questions, along with more details expanding the question, help set up material that in the second part of each

ENCIRCLING

paragraph after the introduction would follow through by explaining solutions. In the above situations, those would be detailed feats that solve problems related to a cheetah or the human liver. Your essay should cover at least three to five problem-solutions, each developed in its own paragraph. On your final rewrite, be sure to employ Flow, Pause, and Fusion to bring alive the reality of everything in the body of your piece. Remember, this is always an important part of writing anything, but it is typically absent in the bland-makes-it-objective style found in many of your sources.

LAYERING

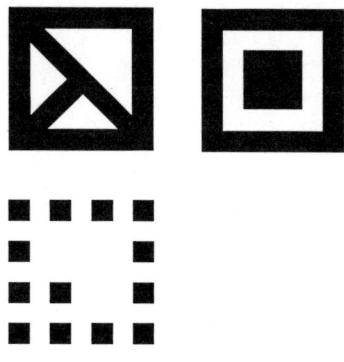

ways to divide

At times an essayist is working with an especially multifaceted, complicated, chunky subject whose depth and breadth squirt in every direction the more the essayist tries to get hold of it. The essayist then needs to fracture this chunkaplex into more manageable pieces without losing its richness. One traditional way to do this is by inventing new cookie cutters that classify items in fresh ways suggested below under Sliced Pie. This allows for a very systematic layering of reality. More complex strategies involve Double Exposures and Thirteen Ways, both of which allow the writer to bring one or more voices or styles into the piece of writing. These strategies are more rarely used, surprising given the latter half of the twentieth century's fascination with deconstruction — viewing reality with a multiple-perspective eye — that has permeated graduate departments in the humanities.

LAYERING 175

Instead of giving writers new layering methods, many deconstructionists encouraged students to jargon-pound material as discussed under Scrub in the Style unit.

SLICED PIE

The Sliced Pie strategy is risky because immature writers often use classification strategies to pigeon-hole or stereotype. There is also the risk of believing or arguing that what is true for one thing is also automatically true about anything similar to it, called the *fallacy of composition*. For instance, what is true about one person is not necessarily true about another one who shares other similar characteristics. Sliced Pie should always be considered an attempt to momentarily capture complexity, not to fossilize it. By temporarily laying a schemata over a complex subject, the reader gains new insight into complex or chaotic subjects. For instance, Edward Hoagland, in his essay "Heaven and Nature," takes on the messy, unpleasant subject of suicide. Hoagland balances the dark, empty-void element of suicide with a frame which orders his insights into a fruitful Sliced Pie. This frame identifies the many types of motivations a person might have for "buying the farm":

> Many suicides inflict outrageous trauma, burning permanent injuries in the minds of their children, though they may have joked beforehand only of "taking a dive." And sometimes the gesture has a peevish or cowardly aspect, or seems to have been senselessly shortsighted as far as an outside observer can tell. There are desperate suicides and crafty suicides, people who do it to cause others trouble and people who do it to save others trouble, deranged exhibitionists who yell from a building

ledge and close-mouthed secretive souls who swim out into the ocean's anonymity. Most of us would prefer not think about why people take their own lives, generalizing suicide into one big, avoidable, messy topic. Hoagland anticipates this anxiety and so Slices the Pie to provide a reassuring framework for the reader that clarifies how the mess really breaks into various understandable, clearly defined reasons for suicide. He could not make such subtle distinctions without employing the Comparison and Contrast Press tool discussed in the Thought unit. This is a key analytical skill for all Sliced Pie writers.

Death also haunts Erik Himmelsbach. After the loss of his mother to cancer, he attempts to make sense of his own estranged relationships to the three men in his and his mother's life, a father and two step-fathers. By subjecting each of the three dads to a characterization and providing specific examples, Himmelsbach is really comparing and contrasting the dads, showing that while each dad may have looked and acted very differently, each of the would-be role models shared the common bond of being incapable of intimate bonding with Erik. Points of contrast and comparison also help provide effective transitions for moving smoothly from type to type. After Himmelsbach gives information about his real father, whom he calls "Biodad," the writer then launches into providing details about his relationship to his mom's second husband, referred to by the writer as "Adoptodad." Himmelsbach uses a point of contrast between the two dads to create a transition from one dad to another: "Whereas Biodad couldn't care less about fatherhood in the conventional sense, Adoptodad did his damnest to fill the void. He was born to play a dad." Using a distinction as a transition wires together the different types while also immediately illustrating one of the cuts that slices the dad pie.

The most successful Sliced Pie essays make careful use of labeling, another technique which causes writer anxiety, since labeling is associated with racism, sexism, and other aspects of stereotyping. In order to separate each dad, Himmelsbach gives them

LAYERING

all creative labels: Biodad, Adoptodad, and Fauxdad. The labels do two things. They help organize the material so that a reader does not confuse dads, and the labels capture an essential quality of that dad, the label itself becoming a mini-thesis, centering the reader for upcoming evidence. For instance, by labeling his real father "Biodad," Himmelsbach suggests a dad who is capable of only a cold, DNA relationship. Descriptive details within the Biodad slice confirms this.

Sliced Pie can also be used as a playground for irreverence or lighter subjects. In its "Shouts and Murmurs" section, *The New Yorker* magazine published a short satiric piece by Betsy Berne called the "Tired Chronicles," a classification of different types of tired people where "the down-trodden poor, who don't have time to discuss the intricacies of fatigue" were immediately excluded. Instead, Berne ironically focuses on upper middle-class types: tired married people with kids; tired single people who work somewhat outside the home and those who work exclusively at home; the international, jet-set tired group. Berne's Sliced Pie makes fun of those lucky people, herself included, who lead comfortable, financially secure, even exciting lives, and who receive a perverse enjoyment from the luxury of complaining about tiredness. The Sliced Pie mode allows Berne to register a complaint about people who complain, an uncorking of the middle class, while keeping her satire in a controlled format.

The social world gets an even more raucus-flavored humored in *Life in Hell* by Matt Groening, the creator of "The Simpsons," who slices up "The 9 Types of Boyfriends," "The 9 Types of Girlfriends," "The 9 Types of Relationships," plus a division of types of teachers from "School is Hell." Groenig characterizes all of them by their advantages, disadvantages, common forms of address, and dialogue. A similar format but with much darker humored , not-for-classroom-use slicing, is used in "Foreigners Around the World" from *The National Lampoon,* written by a younger, much less conservative P.J. O'Rourke. This attack on bigoted world-views works by dividing all people, from Africans to Swiss, into twenty-one ethnic groups; then making fun of stereotypic prejudices about all of them through an offensive point of view that exaggerates racial characteristics, so-called good points, proper forms of address, and anecdotes illustrating character. Although satiric, this piece will choke the politically correct. A sincere, politically correct antidote is "Mother Tongue" by Amy Tan, published in *Threepenny Review*, which is really an anti-Sliced Pie tract. Tan criticizes classification strategies, revealing the problem with people trying to make assumptions based on careless classifications. She dramatizes this by how quickly she changes her own use of language from academic English to broken, English-As-a-Second-Language English which captures the wisdom of her mother.

The academic world is virtually all Sliced Pie. "A Tale of Piggery" by Brian Kelly in *Newsweek* is textbook perfect Sliced Pie about pork-barrel politics excerpted from his *Adventures in Porkland*. Kelly divided Congressional budget favors ranging from the hidden, blatant, justifiable to the silly, by describing them under Rotten Pork, the really laugh-out-loud kind, such as funds for "whether tequila will make fish drunk" studies; Big Pork, Power Pork, Perpetual Pork, Presidential Pork, Academic Pork, Defense Pork, Tax Pork, and People's Pork, which involve titlements. *Break-up: The Core of Modern Art* is a book by Katharine Kuh which slices the art of the twentieth-century off from others because it is "characterized by shattered surfaces, broken color, segmented compositions, dissolving forms and shredded images;" then she subdivides all the movements of modern art: For instance, surrealism is characterized by "splinted time sequence with an abandon borrowed from the world of fragmented dreams" with content "unhinged," "allowing disconnected episodes to recreate the disturbing life of our unconscious."

One of the most helpful Sliced Pies from the world of social science is "Malignant Aggression: Necrophilia," a section in *The Anatomy of Human Destructiveness* by Erich Fromm, who helpfully divides the socio-psychological world into necrophilia and biophilia. In its extreme form, necrophilia is characterized by a desire to sexually abuse corpses, but Fromm sees this as a metaphor for any tendency to transform something that is alive into something stale, including to solve problems with force; to focus on sickness and failure; to react with indifference towards favorable change and others' enthusiasm; to maintain an obsessed attachment with the past, material things, and regulations; to respond to humor with self-consciousness, rather than with spontaneity. Biophilia is the opposite: preference for the new over the certain, molding through love and reason, and believing that good is a reverence for life.

Psychology and sports mix in "Psychiatric Study of Professional Football" in *Saturday Review World* by Arnold Mandell, a psychologist hired by the San Diego Charger football team, who noticed that offensive players, suited to choreographed offensive plans, had neat lockers; defensive players, suited to wrecking those plans, had messy lockers. Mandell noticed other personality traits compatible for the large variety of talents called for by the different positions on both squads. For instance, someone who had toughness more akin to sacrificial stubbornness rather than explosiveness, could best meet the requirements for playing a middle offensive linemen. Mandell used the football positions as metaphors: his mother being an offensive lineman and Woody Allen having the despair and vanity of a wide receiver.

A creative philosophical use of ancient Sliced Pie is part of *Ethica Nicomachea* by the (384-322 B.C.) philosopher Aristotle, who here slices conduct into different activities and then subdivides all of these into two extremes of conduct, one a vice of excess, the other a vice of defect. Happiness exists in a virtuous mean between the two. For example, the mean between the vice of excess, Boastfulness, and the vice of defect, Mock Modesty, is Truth Telling; between the vice of excess, Buffoonery, and the vice of defect, Boorishness, is Ready Wit; between the vice of excess, Rashness, and the vice of defect, Cowardice, is Courage.

WORKOUT: *Take Notes:* Get ready to use Slice Pie with a group of human beings. Do field work and begin taking notes at a place where you work, hang out, or visit often. In choosing a subject, stay clear of using obviously opposed groups such as good students versus bad students or coffee drinkers versus tea drinkers. Distinctions here are too obvious and do not require an essay. A better subject is different types of business students or different types of breakfast eaters, seemingly homogeneous groups which allow the the writer to be more revealing by highlighting subtle distinctions. Try to identify at least four or five sub-categories or types. Begin with the type you know the most about and list all their defining characteristics, using physical traits, examples of behavior, typical language usage, purchases, favorite dishes — include anything that might be important to making telling distinctions with similar items in other groups. When listing traits for the other types, consider parallel details. Glynis wrote a Sliced Pie on coffee drinkers that considered each sub-group's type of coffee drinks, use of cream and sugar, frequency of drinking, the drinkers' appearances, their profession, their dialogue, whether the coffee was to go or enjoyed at a table. You never know what kind of detail will best help define your groups, and sometimes after the first draft you will need to combine two groups because of their similarities or pinch a new sub-group off of one you already created.

Labeling: Once your groups are detailed, come up with interesting labels for each type. It may be helpful to review the chapter on Recyclables, Melted-Together-Words, and Line-Ups in the Style unit, the last two usually functioning as adjectives describing nouns. Using Recyclables, Glynis relabeled her Sliced Pie on Coffee Drinkers as Mud Guzzlers, mud being a slang word for coffee and guzzler being a synonym for drinker. In her draft, Glynis identified a type of coffee drinker, the serious coffee drinker, whom she relabels as the hyper-mud-o-phile, borrowing Greek and Latin to help underscore that group's dominating characteristic.

Ordering: Decide on an effective order for presenting your groups. In "My Three Dads," Himmelsbach uses a chronological order, writing about his three dads in the order they entered his

LAYERING

life. After characterizing Biodad and Adoptodad, but before going on to Faux Dad, Himmelsbach has his Mom get her foot in the door by sketching touching memories where his Mom played the dad role. By placing her pie piece in the middle, her muscling effectiveness as a "dad" stands out when juxtaposed against the other dads' shortcomings. By avoiding the impulse to place the most important "Dad," his Mom, at the end or the beginning of the essay, Himmelsbach pays compliment and homage to his dead mother. Once you have decided on an effective order, make transitions from type to type by using a point of comparison or contrast between the sub-category you are just exiting and the one you are entering as Himmelsbach does described above.

Introductions and conclusions: These should be done last. The best Sliced Pie essays are those that not only carefully classify, but which also make a point or give a reason why they are identifying different types. Hoagland thinks about reasons to commit suicide because he is aging, depressed, and is frightened that he is giving suicide consideration. Himmelsbach reviews his relationships with his various fathers because his mother's death makes him realize that she filled the dad role. Your own introduction can be personal or a general observation but avoid trite openings such as "There are many different types, each with their own characteristics." Also avoid summary conclusions such as, "As you can see, there are many different types of coffee drinkers, but as you can see they all love coffee." For instance, you can Mandell á la mode your Sliced Pie (see Mandell's essay on football above), extending the slices by turning them into metaphorical labels for people you know, celebrities, or historical figures. In any case, gourmet torte slices without ice cream are better than corn-bread-crumb endings.

DOUBLE EXPOSURE

Looking at old family photos gives us an eerie feeling because we are reminded of the dual nature of any reality. There is the reality of the photograph: parents holding their infant at a baptism, a thirteen year old swallowing manhood at his Bar Mitzvah, a high school graduate waving her diploma, newlyweds shading their eyes at the Colosseum in Rome. The viewer sees the costumes, smiles, setting, and other visual clues that help remind everyone of the event. Then there is the hidden reality of the day, the psychological drama hidden from the camera lens: parents embarrassed that their infant urine-soaked the priest, the Bar Mitzvah boy recovering from throwing up a pastrami sandwich at his reception; the graduate's turmoil over her boyfriend going away to a different college; the couple's inability to conceive a child on their Roman holiday.

Aside from the obvious dual nature between the physical, conscious world and the psychological, subconscious world, there are many other dual realities. For instance, a doctor looking at a body notices its mechanical and chemical anatomy and discovers unseen disease and sickness invading that body. However, an artist looking at a body notices shapes, shadows, lines, and colors that might be exaggerated to satirize human vanity. Neither the doctor's nor the artist's view is more valid or "real" than the other, neither interpretation is right or wrong, neither is part of a more positive or negative endeavor, unless one was a murderous cannibal. The two together represent a more rounded view. Capturing this dual reality in a written piece is an exciting challenge for a writer.

For Judy Ruiz, the double layered perspective of her essay

LAYERING 183

"Oranges and Sweet Sister Boy" allows her to write about her mental illness in a format which mirrors her sometimes disjointed or fractured view of reality. Ruiz, who suffers from paranoid schizophrenia, struggles with her own identity while also trying to come to terms with the fact that her brother, who is undergoing a sex change operation, is trying to physically change his identity. Ruiz splits these concerns between two distinctly styled paragraphs which alternate throughout the essay since, as the writer notes, "sometimes dreams get mixed up with not-dreams." In the first version, Ruiz reasons her way through her crisis using a lucid narrative style where events unfold in real time: "I am sleeping, hard, when the telephone rings. It's my brother and he's calling to say he is now my sister." Although the information in the first version is highly personal and extraordinary, the tone remains clear and the style rational.

This first version is juxtaposed by another style text which is distinguished from the first version through the use of a smaller font. In this second version, Ruiz replaces her more rational prose with memories, dreams, and random thoughts which are communicated through a style which uses incomplete sentences — "My Mother. My father," shifting circumstances — conception in Dallas at the same time she is a passing girl, surreal details — "false teeth slipping down," and symbolic references— "the Creators":

> My mother. My father. I am conceived near Dallas in the dark while a child passes, a young girl who knows and doesn't know, who witnesses, in glimpses, the creation of the universe, who feels an odd hurt as her own mother, fat and empty, snores with her mouth open, her false teeth slipping down, snores and snores just two seats behind the Creators.

This second version allows Ruiz to convey disturbing thoughts and past events that would lose their gnarled timbre in a more traditional prose style. Yet, the reader can only unknot and interpret the ideas and images in the second version by relying on clues communicated in the first version. In Ruiz's essay, the two versions operate together to help the writer decode her hidden thoughts and troubling memories. Ruiz's use of the Double Exposure helps to underscore her divided feelings over her brother becoming her sister. This ambiguity is reflected in Ruiz's conclusion: "Something in me says no to all this, and that this surgery business is the ultimate betrayal of the self. And yet, I want my brother to be happy." Ruiz's Double Exposure reminds her reader that often we deal with serious difficulties through a complicated blend of our reason and intuition.

In her article "Boobs in Toyland," published in *The Village Voice*, Gwen Blair is sensitive to the dual nature of reality when she writes her article on the Barbie Doll. On the one hand, Blair nods to the historical, economic, and sociological view of the Barbie phenomenon. Most of the body of Blair's essay is an academic account and analysis of the history and development of the famous doll: We learn that since its inception, one plastic doll has been produced for every female in the United States and Canada; that Ruth Handler invented Barbie after watching her own daughter, named Barbie, play with adult fashion dolls; that Handler teamed with her husband who was a plastics expert to fashion a mature-figured doll, pooling all their savings to run commercials on the 1950's Mickey Mouse show and that sales reach over $7 billion dollars a year.

Yet Blair knows that there is another Barbie reality, one having to do with her owner's secret, private fantasies. In order to allow this reality to speak every few paragraphs, the more academic reality is intersected by testimonies and confessions of women in their twenties who played with Barbie as young girls. In these italicized versions, we get shocking testimonies that would never surface in an academic paper. From Delores, 29, artist: *I never really liked Barbie. I thought she was snippy and bitchy and when she sat down all she could do was stick her legs straight out. Still, she was so much better than my mother . . .* From Paula, 23, a secretary, just after the primary text's reasoned voice mentions that "Barbie also served as a focus for her owner's insecurities, frustrations, and fears": *I resented that Barbie always looked just right, no matter what I did to her, and I was*

LAYERING 185

always a mess. And it was so irritating to look at those blank bumps that were her breasts. There was nothing to identify with. First I drew in nipples. Then I bashed them on my night side table. When the primary text coolly points out that Barbie and her male counterpart, Ken, also "provided a certain outlet for her owner's sexual curiosity," another double exposure gets to the bottom line: *I wasn't sure who was on top and who was on the bottom, so instead Ken and Barbie had sex flying through the air. Once I used Ken to masturbate, but then I felt guilty. I was afraid he'd remember.* The two realities, one academic, the other intimate, both distinct in style and the type of information given, compliment one another to create a whole picture, leaving the reader knowing that without both, reality would have been cheated.

Doubles Exposures can also be humorous, such as in "Gender Gap: It's in the Genes," in *The Los Angeles Times*, by Beth Ann Krier and Jeannine Stein. The primary exposure discusses the differences between the attitudes of men and women shoppers, including their purposes and methodology, while a second reality is represented by different stand-up routines from well known comics. "Anguilo's Republic," in *New England Monthly* and compiled by Robert Bertsche, is a compilation of quotes by the Boston mob boss, Gennaro Anguilo, recorded by the FBI. The quotes are Double Exposed with quick, cliché, classical headings used by great thinkers from antiquity and the Age of Reason. The contrast, between these wisdom-flags and Anguilo's gutter remarks, is a killer: On The Meaning Of Time — "Time marches on! Time waits for no one. I got the f------ hole burning in my f-----" brain!" or On Prudence — "When a guy knocks ya down, never get up unless he's gonna kill ya."

More deadly Double Exposures include "The Day the Bomb Went Off; an Imaginary Event," in *The Progressive*, by Erwin Knoll and Theodore Postol, written in 1978 when nuclear obliteration seemed eminent. Both exposures are written with objectivity, but one version imagines the flesh-and-blood effects of a twenty-megaton nuclear bomb explosion on specific neighborhoods in the Chicago area; the second, italicized version coldly explains the scientific facts. The contrast is chilling. "The Killing Game" in *Esquire* by Joy Williams Double-Exposes the verbal style of hunting magazines, represented in italics, with her own anti-hunting sarcasm, turning hunters' entries into self-damnation. For instance, "The animal becomes the property of the hunter by its death. Alive, the beast belongs only to itself. This is unacceptable to the hunter. *He's yours ... He's mine ... I decided to ... I decided not to ... I debated shooting it, then I decided to let it live ..."* Or in discussing hunting technology: "They use sex lures ... *The big buck raised its nose to the air, curled back its lips, and tested the scent of the doe's urine. I held my breath, fought back the shivers, and jerked off a shot."*

WORK OUT: Pick any subject to write on such as an important political event, a classroom experience, a scientific discovery, a business transaction, an architectural creation, or a parent. Pick a subject that you know exists in two realms of reality, one an official version and the other a more intimate version, one more literal and the other more spiritual, one more scientific and one more flesh-and blood, or one more serious and one more humorous. Both versions must be informative, well supported by details, and underscored with an appropriate, consistent style. This is not a pro and con strategy or intelligent view versus stupid view tic-tac-toe. You must feel that both versions are credible and meaningful.

Do not use any transitions when you cut back and forth, but do place the parts of both versions that seem to have related material close to each other. One exposure should be double spaced and one either single spaced or written in italics or both. Move from version one to version two, and back to version one, at least once per page or else there will not be enough of a Double Exposure effect. On the other hand, do not cut back and forth more than twice per page — from version one to version two, back to version one and two — or else the piece usually becomes too complicated to read. Many students find it easier to write two papers and then splice them together into one.

LAYERING

THIRTEEN WAYS
■ ■ ■ ■
■   ■
■ ■   ■
■ ■ ■ ■

"Thirteen Ways of Looking at a Blackbird" is a poem by the well-known American poet and insurance executive, Wallace Stevens. The poem looks at blackbirds in thirteen different ways, through thirteen very short stanzas, written in thirteen different styles to capture a more complete picture on what blackbirds signify than would be possible with a poem written from one perspective, in one voice, through one style. In Stevens's poem, one stanza has a prophetic tone that makes the bird a reminder of down-to-earth, feminine intuition as opposed to masculine, idealistic illusions ("O thin men of Haddam,/ Why do you imagine golden birds?/ Do you not see how the blackbird/ Walks around the feet/ Of the women about you?"); another seems more like a haiku depicting the bird as a lively observant force countering vast, static forces in the world ("Among twenty snowy mountains/ The only moving thing/ Was the eye of the blackbird."); one is in a folk tale format to dramatize the bird as a figment of the threatened imagination ("He rode over Connecticut / In a glass coach./ Once, a fear pierced him,/ In that he mistook/ The shadow of his equipage/ For blackbirds."); another is written like a mathematical equation where the bird completes a trinity that includes the abstract forces that bind two people ("A man and a woman and a blackbird/ Are one.")

Just as with "Thirteen Ways of Looking at a Blackbird," Thirteen Ways is a strategy that fragments into more than Double Exposure's two layers of reality, but the writer does not keep returning to each layer; so Thirteen Ways cannot develop any one angle as completely as Double Exposure. However, the variety and number of fragments allows for more far-ranging perspectives, voices, tones, and lengths than Double Exposures. Each fragment can range from one word to several paragraphs and also can be argumentative, defining, narrative, satirical, in fact, involve any of the styles and organizational strategies listed in this book. This fragmentation nourishes the variable parts of any multi-faceted, complex subject.

The strategy also drives a stake through the tendency for any writer to lapse into the *either-or fallacy* (also referred to as *false dilemma* of *fallacy of bifurcation*) which is an approach to writing, or life, that argues a point of view by assuming there are only two positions or conclusions to take, one of which is usually depicted as unattractive. The favored one might ultimately be the truthful one, but not by virtue of there being only one other unattractive alternative. Just as not all political realities can be reduced to one for-or-against issue, not all characters in fiction are either only strong or weak; not all portrait subjects are either only happy or sad; not all attachments to possessions either greedy or pragmatic; not all emotional attractions either only rational or irrational. Aside from being something in between these extremes, reality presents other ironies: supporting something can squash something else desirable; intellectual strengths can lead to downfalls; intense happiness can melt into melancholia. All of life's endeavors — artistic, technological, interpersonal, political, economic — usually center around paradox and ambiguity.

In the essay world, Thirteen Ways's use of fragmentation to energize the truth seems very unconventional, but it is nothing new. Art historian E.H. Gombrich argues that ancient Egyptian artists worried much more about completeness than smooth transitions, not painting what could be seen at a given moment from a single point of view, but rather painting all important angles at once. For instance, the totality of a human's eye, its circumference and shape, can be seen most completely from a frontal view; the other facial features, arms, and leg movements are more vivid from a profile angle; so for accuracy's sake, the Egyptians combined frontal and profile views. They were not concerned with creating illusions more comfortable to the eye, but with ensuring accurate identification of a person so the gods could make correct soul-identification after the depicted person died. Many art

LAYERING 189

critics see modern cubism as this same attempt to transcend the illusion of visual perspective which is limited to a single point of view, possible only at a single point in time, by incorporating several angles of view from different times — from the top, front, back, or sides — all in one view at one time. In the twentieth century, hundreds of modern creators such as Cezanne, Chagal, Picasso, Faulkner, Joyce, Woolfe, Barthleme, even architects such as Frank Gehrey, undercut the *Ego Es Ibi* or I-am-there fallacy, the assumption that a work of art should be primarily judged on its ability to create one-point-perspective verisimilitude. There are many more ways to appreciate creative works than solely on their fulfillment of people's desire to have an illusion that is so real that "they are there."

There are other strong justifications for Thirteen Ways. "Making the Eye a Better Witness" by Edwin Chen in the *The Los Angeles Times* covers the work of UCLA psychologists who discovered that eyewitness accounts of crimes become much more accurate when witnesses are asked to not just describe what happened, but to describe their own frame of mind at the time, reconstruct the crime in a variety of time sequences other than from only beginning to end, and to recreate the incident from the criminal's perspective as well as their own. In short, witnesses most accurately interpret reality creating a Thirteen Ways, eye-witness portfolio. "World View" by Barry Starvo, also for *The Los Angeles Times*, demonstrates that it is impossible to depict the globe accurately in a two dimensional map. He reviews six versions of the globe popular at different times, including Buckminster Fuller's fold-out map, and explains how each inevitably exaggerates different visual qualities with different political implications, all visualizing some aspects of reality and none ever totally encircling it completely. The maps taken together create a topographical Thirteen Ways.

Peter Blaunder wrote an article entitled "New York Style" for *New York* magazine by compiling seventy-nine stanza-like viewpoints on New York style, effectively Egyptianizing the reality of the city in a manner impossible to accomplish in a more unified, easy-on-the-mind's-eye essay. Blaunder compiles the diverse points of views, articulated through disparate styles, without smooth transitions, the dramatic jolts between entries reminding the reader that the complexity of New York style can only be captured through radical shifts of perspectives.

Some of the entries focus on bizarre juxtapositions and paradoxes such as Annie Flanders who said, "Tuxedos in the daytime and sunglasses at night. Earning off the books and learning on the job. Being invited to a party you can't get into and getting into a party you weren't invited to. A pair of worn jeans and a $900 belt. A limo to the airport and a budget flight to Rome. Downtown luring uptown and uptown luring downtown. Dressing white in winter and dressing black in summer. Not caring and caring desperately. Makeup on boys and crew cuts on girls. Nine to five P.M. and nine to five A.M. New York." Without transition, other entries cut in that are very simple, such as Isaac Bashevis Singer's one word entry, "RUSH." Other entries are more metaphorical such as John Chancelor's: "The avenues in my neighborhood are Pride, Covetousness, and Lust; the cross streets are Anger, Gluttony, Envy, and Sloth. I live over on Sloth, and the style on our street is to avoid the other thoroughfares."

Like Stevens's glass coach stanza, some entries are mini-drama's. Consider David Mamet's: "I was down in the village recently on a very rainy day when a cab pulled up at a light. A young man and a woman started to get out with their baby as the light turned green, and a second car pulled up behind them. The man in the second car got out and started yelling, 'Are you out of your fucking mind? Are you out of your fucking mind?' That is New York style." In contrast to humorous dramas, some entries are touching images of cultural integration. James Morton, Dean of St. John the Divine, remembers a forty foot Christmas tree with unusual decorations, "2,000 origami paper cranes folded by New York school children as part of a traditions started in Hiroshima by an eleven-year-old girl who was dying from radiation and made the first such cranes on her deathbed."

A similar layering of a city, more focused on political tension than style, is a Thirteen Ways entitled "Jerusalem — Fall 1990" by Aaron Back in *Tikkun: A Bimonthly Jewish Critique of Politics, Culture & Society* discovered in Harper's Magazine. The piece was written two months after the Iraqi invasion of Kuwait. It is built of various vignettes that describe the wide ranging reactions of the author and people to one another in various types of encounters after three Israelis were stabbed to death by Palestinians revenging Palestinians killed earlier on the Temple Mount. One vignette describes a landlady who shows sincere personal concern at one moment and raises rent fifty percent the next; another a Lamaze class filled with talk of calming babies while one friend argues that blowing up houses to punish people is no worse than losing a house through foreclosure in the United States.

Other tastes of Thirteen Ways are often centered on creative choice and its implications. Margaret Atwood's "Women's Novels" in *Likely Stories: A Postmodern Sampler* and "Not-Knowing" by Donald Barthelme, use multiple entries to capture all the angles that develop a fictional work. *Sketch book with Voices* by Eric Fischl, with Jerry Saltz, was reprinted in *Harper's Magazine* at the time of Fischl's retrospective at The Whitney Museum. This compilation captures the essence of contemporary art by including an exercise or admonition from different artists on each page of the sketchbook: Chuck Close says, "Make a painting in which every part of the painting is of equal importance," while Cindy Sherman' demands, "Do your own work, but use someone else's clothes," and Jennifer Bartlett's reveal the psychological, "In the morning make long lists of things to do. In the afternoon write down whose ideas they were." Taking the commercial aspects of creativity into consideration, syndicated columnist Art Buchwald, in "And Just What Is a Newspaper Editor," describes the editor from his own point of view, then the reporter's point of view, then the publisher's, and finally the syndicated columnist's, who, of course, sees the editor as "forthright, brave, intelligent, and honorable, . . . a credit to his profession and race" for choosing the piece in the first place. Buchwald's essay has Thirteen-Ways spirit, but stays in one humorous voice. Thirteen Ways can layer a person's life or a type of person's reality. *The 100th Boyfriend* is a compilation by Bridget Daly and Janet Skeels that includes one hundred viewpoints and voices on boyfriends: one written as a catalog of attributes ("Joe polished the bottoms of the Revere ware pans once a month ... Joe thought I looked good in shorts as long as I didn't walk too fast ... Joe was the kind of man you take home to your parents and leave there"), one looking for common denominators in boyfriends, finally shocked that it "was bad eyesight," one laden with metaphors, including replaying the tape machine to listen to the boyfriend's voice, "sucking on those vowels," and ninety-seven others. Camille Paglia's "The Diana Cult" for *The New Republic* is focused on only one person, does not shift styles in each section of the essay, but is fractured into different "archetypal" perspectives, regarding England's Princess Diana as Cinderella, the betrayed wife, the princess in the tower, the mater dolorosa, the pagan goddess, the Hollywood queen, the beautiful boy.

WORKOUT: Pick a subject that you feel is so large and complicated that it would be more honest to write about it through jolting, multiple angles than through a smoothly transitioned, single-perspective essay. Possibilities include a complex work of artistic merit, a city, a person, money, education, a philosophical viewpoint.

You should have a minimum of eight ways of looking at your subject. Some may be heavily metaphoric and others academic; some very short and others more developed; some focused on a specific detail and others making insightful generalities; some mini-dramas and others analytic; some humorous and others very serious; some spiritual and others down-to-earth. Remember that any of the other stylistic and organizational patterns discussed in this book can give you ideas on how to think and write one of your paragraph stanzas.

LAYERING

Be sure that each of your paragraph stanzas works well by itself. Sometimes students include filler entries that are shallow, written from a narrow person's point of view, or lacking in specifics and careful style. Some of the samples above are compilations which made the writer's job easier. You can also get ideas from other people, but you must think they are legitimate. Mold and shape them so they are distinct and communicate clearly, and accept them as your own. Every entry must fill in a crucial angle. In order to prepare your reader for the dramatic shifts between entries, it is best to number your entries by placing the number of each stanza in the middle of the page, double space, and then write the next entry.

UNCORKING

ways to disarm

Disarming an opposing view-point by revealing its absurdity or highlighting its hypocrisy, presents special challenges for the essayist. If the essayist's unbridled passion becomes overwhelming, there is the risk of committing critical thinking fallacies. For instance, being enraged births the *ad hominem* fallacy, attacking the opponent's personal attributes rather than the details of the opponent's position. Other electrically charged essayists, attacking issues by appealing to their reader's emotional vulnerability — for instance on death penalty, animal rights, abortion issues — often commit the *ad misercordium* fallacy, justifying a position by arousing the reader's sense of pity rather than sense of reason. On the other hand, approaching a charged issue with a gutted attitude and a flat voice suffocates the sincere conviction necessary to disarm a point of view already barricaded with its own use of fallacies.

UNCORKING

Satire, exaggeration, and ironic points-of-view are often overlooked as some of the most effective devices for enabling the essayist to passionately argue a case without running the risk of overindulging the emotions. A tongue-in-cheek tone demands control. The ironic or satiric voice uncorks an opponent's position by making the same points covered in a straightforward argument; however, the points carry more weight because the distinct, satiric tone jerks the reader's eyes open. Since hitting the ironic note requires concentration and careful modulation of voice, running amuck is avoided, and there is little risk of letting emotions roam too freely.

We have found that in order to uncork successfully, writing students must work within a clearly defined format which can support a combo load of passion, sarcasm, and wit. Devil's Advice, Mocking with Mass Media, and the more subtle uses of "Are You Talking to Me?" and Sincerely Yours, provide hardware which can accommodate the weight of a charged tone. In order to argue effectively, you will find it helpful to review the Scrub section under the Style unit since a target's language is usually swollen with euphemism, and pricking it can always be a part of bringing the opponent down to reality.

DEVIL'S ADVICE

Strong proposals rely on some or all of the five basic methods for putting together an argumentative piece: supporting with facts and statistics, citing authorities, offering examples, answering objections by the opposition, predicting consequences. Sometimes, when relying on these methods alone, we find ourselves unintentionally "preaching to the congregation," our argument reaching only the ears of those who already favor our position. No matter how well a position is argued, it is very difficult to get the opposition's attention: facts and statistics bore, and skeptics know they can be manipulated; authorities can be fatted with self-interest; predictions can appear to be guess work or empty threats; the opposition can always claim to be misunderstood. Most of all, an opponent's self-righteousness is formidable protective armor against any rationale argument. Devil's Advice penetrates this armor.

First of all, Devil's Advice seduces the opponent by appearing to be agreeable. However, this agreement is ironic. Devil's Advice slices through an opponent's argument by humorously exaggerating the opponent's hidden motives and illogic into an overblown, formal proposal, bringing the negative aspects of the argument into an intense light for others to scrutinize. Since the essayist is creating a proposal that he or she does not truly believe in, Devil's Advice is tongue-in-cheek humor. The tongue-in-cheek praise and advice advocated by the ironic proposal confuses the opponent, puts the opponent off guard, and raises the spirits of readers victimized by the opponent's self-importance.

In 1729 Jonathan Swift published "A Modest Proposal," one of the iciest pieces of Devil's Advice ever written, a pamphlet that pretended to be a logical proposal for a "fair, cheap, and easy method" to deal with the "prodigious number of children" in Ireland. In actuality, Swift intends to create sympathy for the oppressed, hungry, Irish Catholic peasants, and focus anger on wealthy, bigoted, English absentee landlords and the English aristocrats whose government silently let the Irish bleed.

In the "modest," logical tone of a benevolent social planner, Swift's persona proposed a plan whereby Irish children instead of "wanting food and raiment for the rest of their lives . . . shall on the contrary contribute to the feeding, and partly to the clothing, of many thousands." The plan would also prevent voluntary abortions, a sacrifice "which would move tears and pity in the most savage and inhuman breast." After a careful analysis of how much it costs to raise a child to the first year, and careful, realistic calculations on how many Irish women are "breeders," Swift gets to the bottom line which he hopes "will not be liable to the least objection": "I have been assured by a very knowing American of my acquaintance in London, that a young healthy child well nursed is at a year old a most delicious, nourishing, and wholesome food, whether stewed, roasted, baked, or boiled; and I make no doubt that it will equally serve in a fricassee or a ragout."

The proposal, like all good proposal arguments, outlines the results and methods of the plan: "a child will make two dishes at an entertainment for friends;" "the fore or hind quarter will make a reasonable dish . . . boiled on the fourth day;" infant's flesh will be in season all year long, but especially in March because "there are more children born in Roman Catholic countries about nine months after Lent;" the carcass may be skinned to make "admirable gloves for ladies, and summer boots for fine gentlemen;" and finally, although it would help to replace the abuses of deer hunting, allowing adolescents into the meat supply would not be recommended since boys would be a tough chew and girls would not be far from becoming breeders themselves.

With the same steadiness, Swift's persona outlines the advantages of the proposal, including that "men would become as fond of their wives during the time of their pregnancy as they were now of their mares in foal, their cows in calf, or sows when they are ready to farrow." Near the end of the essay, he asks anyone who thinks he has a better proposal to first ask the miserable Irish if they do not agree whether they would have been better off sold as food at a year old since he is sure the answer is "yes." Finally, lest anyone think Swift's persona has a personal interest in the plan, he points out that he does not have his own "children by which I can propose to get a single penny."

Swift's essay is successful because he develops what he knows are hidden and not-so-hidden hatreds for the Irish, formalizing those hatreds into a proposal so grim that no one would want to claim support for them. In fact, the grotesqueness of Swift's essay dominates any discussion about the Irish so strongly that people who wished to voice any anti-Irish opinions would hesitate, knowing they risked getting some of Swift's essay splattered all over themselves. Mark Twain often set up the same kind of dilemma for his reader or listener. For instance, in his "Advice to Youth," an address to students, he smoked out their hidden corruptions through an outrageous proposal to learn good lie telling since "many a young person has injured himself permanently through a single clumsy and ill-finished lie, the result of carelessness born of incomplete training." Twain's "advice" includes details on how to manipulate parents and become good conformists.

In a slightly different use of the strategy called "No Wonder They Call Me a Bitch," Ann Hodgman, a contributing editor to *Spy* magazine, describes spending "the better part of a week eating dog food" in order to verify dog food advertising claims. She turns on the skillet, cooks up Gaines-burgers, samples "a piece of red extrusion," the patty "leaking rivulets of red dye." After lining up seven flavors of Milk-Bone Flavor Snacks on the floor in order to make gourmet decisions about which to eat, she realizes "Unless my dog's palate is a lot more sensitive than mine — and considering that she steals dirty diapers out of the trash and eats them, I'm loath to think it is — she doesn't detect any more difference in the seven flavors than I did when I tried them." Hodgman's writes gut-punching Devil's Advice by actually describing herself carrying out her outrageous proposal.

It is difficult to find many pure tastes of Devil's Advice, and we hope students will revive this classic satiric form. A good example is "Miracle Drug" by student Gregory Bedford, who gives Devil's Advice restoring the benefits of cocaine, including "increased awareness of financial matters, heightened creativity, and sharpened social skills." Financial advantages include developing very prudent spending habits to keep up with the cost

UNCORKING

of cocaine, which means trimming non-essentials such as "food, medicine, and hygiene products" since coke's numbing effects "will hide from the body any symptoms of approaching illness" and nose-numbness make soap and deodorant irrelevant.

WORKOUT: First you need to pick a target: a politician, an employer or teacher, an organization or institution, a relative or friend who has betrayed you. Then you need to sniff out and make a list of all the target's immoral, hidden motives and the illogic of its not-so-hidden positions. You need facts about your opponent, so you may need to do some research.

Now you are ready for the rough draft. Instead of arguing against these stupidities, first exaggerate them by making the opponent's wishes even more extreme or outlandish, smoking out what your opponent could never admit to even to himself. Now, "support" these horrors. Support them by formalizing them into a well developed proposal and by standing on your opponent's soap box, not your own. Allow the absurd to be show-cased. Keep a cool, steady voice, and without flinching, propose embarrassing desires and illogical solutions. Write as if you expect praise rather than contempt, but of course what you offer is worthy of contempt. Remember to consider all the components of a well argued proposal outlined above in the first sentence of Devil's Advice. The juxtaposition of your outrageous proposal, packaged in the competent, traditional components of a business or persuasive essay proposal, will create a tongue-in-cheek satiric essay.

There is one more important thing that we find students forget to do. Even though the essay is agreeing with an outrageous version of the opponent's position, some extremists could still find the proposal acceptable. You must sneak in enough negatives to make sure readers find your proposal unacceptable. One way to sneak these in is to mention the downside of your proposals, but either act as if they are of minor importance, or give outlandish reasons why they are beneficial. For instance, make an outlandish claim in favor of groups that believe government interferes with our personal lives too much: "The government needs to start undoing all those laws it has made that interfere with our every day personal choices, such as seat belt laws." Follow with grotesque results, but with an excuse: "If we take seat belts off of children, sure there will be some kids thrown out the front window and run over, but remember, the world is over-populated." What you praise or advise will be too outlandish for anyone to accuse you of really believing. Anyone who does, deserves to be confused.

COOL DOWN: Review the Scrub section under Style. Consider inflating parts of your proposal by creating euphemisms or terminology for various steps, stages, items, or actions. In other words, try using euphemism as a way of making your proposal more official.

MOCKING WITH MEDIA

Another way to uncork the cliché arguments of a particular group's mentality is to make that mentality absurd and then subject it to the typical, stereotypic devices of a communications form not usually used for that subject matter. This communications form could be a local newspaper, business newsletter, personal ad page, legal brief, restaurant criticism, travel book, or any other written format that has become standardized. Gary understood what makes this concept work while studying a piece entitled "God Is Dead in Georgia" written by Anthony Towne, written originally for *Motive* magazine of the United Methodist Church. Some students always think the essay is an attack on religion, but most see it as an attack on God's "massive diminishing influence," on people who see God and the Trinity only in materialis-

UNCORKING 201

tic and political terms. By using a stereotypic newspaper style to report on such an unlikely event, Towne also makes fun of that style since its seams and gimmicks cannot hold the weight of the the piece's content, God's death. Mocking with Mass Media is always a twofold attack, undercutting a philosophical point of view and ripping a standardized writing format.

For instance, in "God Is Dead in Georgia," Towne squeezes as many credentials as possible into a freighting sentence, typical of some newspapers: "God, creator of the universe, principal deity of the world's Jews, ultimate reality of Christians, and most eminent of all divinities, died late yesterday during major surgery undertaken to correct a massive diminishing influence." Towne uses newspaper inclusion of trivial details with what are at best secondary people, here including a long list of famous theologians and their universities as the assisting "unsuccessful" surgeons. He includes stock newspaper narrowing on the most cliché public relations responses: "The Pope, in Rome, said, in part: 'We are deeply distressed for we have suffered an incalculable loss. The contributions of God to the Church cannot be measured, and it is difficult to imagine how we shall proceed without Him.'" Also the reader finds typical newspaper coverage of only the most worn out, non-threatening responses of people on the street: "'At least he's out of his misery,'" comments a supermarket housewife.

Towne uses legal, flank-protecting language typical of newspapers' concern to avoid responsibility for positions and sources, such as there being "unconfirmed" reports that Jesus, "sometimes" called the Christ, "reputed" son of God, will assume the authority, "if not" the title, of the deceased God, and that "the case is complicated by the fact that Jesus, although he died," was resurrected "so may have not died at all." Finally Towne includes diversions attending to other parts of the newspaper and "human interest" notations to turn serious, complex notions into souvenir-shop items and financial concerns. For instance, the stock market drops sharply until traders get wind that Jesus, "see 'Man in the News,' p. 36, col. 4 — who survives, plans to assume a larger role in the management of the universe." The newspaper promises an upcoming "24-page full-color supplement with many photographs reviewing God's long reign," and requests "pertinent letters, photographs, visions and the like" from the readership.

A slew of other mockings on the same subject showed up years later in "He's Back!!!" edited by Lewis Lapham for Harper's Magazine, all mocking different promotional formats people easily believe in, and again mocking those who assign Jesus political and celebrity worth. Ron Suskind wrote a typical advance memo for Jesus: "DAY ONE—Theme: Traditional values. In reintroducing You, we don't want to create converts so much as tap existing support. To evoke a yearning for simpler days (from A.D. 1 through Eisenhower), it is important to rely on those oft-recited parable. Of course, they'll need to be reworked (boiled to thirty seconds, max) . . ." Al Franken writes Jesus's monologue for "Saturday Night Live;" Gerry Howard at Norton redoes a dust jacket for *The New Testament,* clothes designer Adele Lutz works out wardrobe notes for official meetings, street meetings, and stadium dates; Phyllis Robinson mocks storyboard formats for a one-minute television commercial announcing Jesus's arrival. These are all good formats for mocking other subjects.

The legal world and standardized violent ploys of animated cartoons are just as ripe for Mocking With Mass Media as public relations and religious narrowness. A pure taste of Mocking With Mass Media happens in "Coyote v. Acme" by Ian Frazier, for *The New Yorker,* which makes both legal briefs and violent gimmicks in "Road Runner" cartoons come apart when Wile E. Coyote goes after Acme Company, defendant for "personal injuries, loss of business income, and mental suffering" due to "gross negligence" of products purchased from Acme to catch prey. Premature detonation of one product results in several disfigurements to Mr. Coyote including "severe singeing of the hair on the head, neck, and muzzle" as well as ear fracture, "causing the ear to dangle" with a "creaking sound."

UNCORKING 203

The key to successful satiric mimicking is to compile a list of all the typical stylistic and organizational devices that have turned any language format into a formula so they are no longer sincere, fresh written articulations. The satiric writer makes sure to use everything in this list. The format's worn writing devices will tear open once the fabric of the piece is stressed by the load of outlandish subject matter or content which the essayist is also attacking. The subject matter itself gets the wind punched out of it, not only because of its outlandishness, but because it looks more absurd when it is pressed into the cliché restrictions of the writing format. Both style and subject magnify each other, rendering each other ridiculous. Mocking with Mass Media is a symbiotic satire.

Some Mocking with Mass Medias can even be unintentional. "The Right Jail" by an anonymous author for *M: The Civilized Man* was published by the editors of *Harper's Magazine,* who saw its unintentional humor. This is a guide to minimum-security federal prisons used for wealthy or celebrity white-collar convicts that inadvertently mocks both travel books and the comforts of these prisons. Prisons are starred, with Allenwood getting four since "Accommodations" are superior, "Cuisine" excellent with a "variety of choices at every meal, salad and fruit bar at lunch and dinner, kosher and vegetarian meals," "Work" decent, producing oak and walnut desks for government officials of GS-15 rank; "Ambience and amenities" include a full law library, computers, tennis courts. Then there is one star Maxwell. No vegetarian meals here.

The world of academia is ripe for Mocking With Mass Media. "Deconstructing Willie: The Taco as Imperialist Symbol" for *Texas Monthly* by Stephen Harrigan was picked up by the *Utne Reader.* It spoofs deconstruction literary theory by subjecting a Taco Bell television commercial, featuring Willie Nelson, to the jargonesque thinking that chokes English department graduate departments. The commercial supposedly carries deep significance, such as the taco becoming a symbol of "rapacious imperialism," since in the empty shell "we see the sad defeat of the maize culture that once flourished in the American Eden." "Fabrizio's: Criticism and Response" by Woody Allen, in *The New Yorker*, mocks literary reviews, particularly restaurant reviews, as well as responses to the editor: "One lovely touch at Fabrizio's is Spinelli's Boneless Chicken Parmigiana. The title is ironic, for he has filled the chicken with extra bones, as if to say life must not be ingested too quickly or without caution. . . . One is reminded at once of Webern, who seems to crop up all the time in Spinelli's cooking."

What could be a mocking of trivial research papers, and definitely of American gullibility, happens in "A Neglected Anniversary (The Bathtub Hoax)" by H. L. Mencken included in his *The Bathtub Hoax & Other Blasts and Bravos*. It is a faked, but well "researched," history of the bathtub including "facts" such as "the first American bathtub was installed and dedicated so recently as December 20, 1842 ..." and "in England in 1828 by Lord John Russell." Some Cincinnatians resist the tub at first, the bathtub being "an epicurean and obnoxious toy from England, designed to corrupt the democratic simplicity of the republic." The medical profession worries about "zymotic diseases." Mencken later admitted researching the real history of the tub would be a "dreadful job."

WORKOUT: You need to pick two targets. First decide what political, social, economic, or philosophical position you want to render ridiculous. Make a list of items or positions that you want to cover about this target. Then decide on a language format you would like to target. We have had students go after public television pledge break formats, letters offering insurance and credit card deals, musicals, legal briefs, travel books and articles, scholarly journal writing. Now make a list of at least ten of the organizational and stylistic devices used by this target. If you pick a certain type of newspaper article, the list we have made about Towne's article above may suffice.

Now the two targets must be brought together. First create an outlandish event. For instance, if Towne had wished to attack the clichéd, simplistic attitudes men and women hold for one another, then the headline for the article would be "Men and Women Divide the Earth," or if attacking environmental negligence, the headline might read "Scientists Announce the End of the Sun Is Tomorrow." Use the outlandish situation to explore all the related issues and details of your target. You must write using all ten of the devices from your list that are characteristic of the communications device you also wish to unravel.

"ARE YOU TALKING TO ME?"

The phrase "point of view" can mean two things. It can refer to the philosophical position of a person, or it can refer to the position of the writer with the reader. In the latter sense, point of view can be first person (I, we), or second person (you), or third person (he, she, it, they). Often when we get in an argument, we are quick to talk about our own philosophical point view through first person point of view: "I think this, and I think that." Writers often overlook the advantages of disarming by considering second person and third person points of view.

Second person: When we suddenly realize that another person is not seriously listening to us, we tend to raise our voices in an attempt to capture the listener's attention, and sometimes we even have to fight the temptation to raise our forefinger and point it directly at the other person's face. When making a plea in a written piece, an essayist figuratively finger-points without social-breeching by addressing the reader as "you." Using the second person, a writer establishes an intimate, I-am-right-next-to-you relationship with the reader, pulling the reader inside of the essay, as opposed to pushing the reader away, as when the essay is written from the first person or third person point of view. A sentence written in first person — "I am having a private thought" — allows readers to observe something intimate without imagining themselves to be in the writer's place. A sentence written in the third person — "He and she are having private thoughts." — allows both the reader and writer to look in from the outside. Strong writers know that switching to the second person point of view — "You are having a private thought." — is an effective way of jumping off the page and pulling the reader in by the shirt or blouse collar.

In her essay "Save the Whales, Screw the Shrimp" for *Esquire* magazine, Joy Williams draws attention by finger pointing right from the start of her essay: "I don't want to talk about *me*, of course, but it seems as though far too much attention has been lavished on you lately—that your greed and vanities and quest for self fulfillment have been catered to far too much. You just want and want and want." By avoiding reference to her target in the third person "they" — "They just want and want and want." — which would allow Williams's readers to escape responsibility, Williams uncorks hypocritical Yuppies who compulsively consume yet want to think of themselves as environmentally conscientious. Williams's audience, eager to acquit themselves of any blame or wrongdoing, read on, only to find that they are the target of William's accusations.

Aside from Williams's use, there are other compelling ways to use second person. One is to use the imperative form where "you" is implied through a command, such as "Turn the knob; turn off the lights." This imperative voice is most commonly associated with instruction manuals or process essays which explain how to perform a particular task, such as baking a cake. When used for non-process forms of expository writing, the effect can be dramatic. Whereas Williams uses the second person "you" form to force the reader to take responsibility for his or her actions, another writer, Danna Schaeffer, uses the imperative finger-pointing to help the reader have compassion for her subject, prosecutor Marcia Clark.

UNCORKING

Aside from her infamous role as the lead O.J. Simpson prosecutor, Clark also successfully prosecuted the murderer of actress Rebecca Schaeffer, Danna Schaeffer's daughter. Danna Schaeffer wrote an essay entitled "How to Be Marcia Clark" in *Mirabella* magazine, using the "you" voice to capture Clark's complicated persona. Schaeffer begins her essay on Clark with "Yell when you are born. Don't grow up rich. Learn to work hard and crave victory. Do well in school. Develop an Old Testament sense of justice. Turn into a beautiful woman but don't think of yourself as sexy. Marry someone who's not right for you. Go to law school and discover your fabulous memory stands you in perfect stead. Finish law school. Divorce. Marry again. Take a job with a criminal-defense firm."

Schaeffer knows many of her female readers who watched the trial disapprove of Clark. Anticipating her audience's unwillingness to "relate to" the sharp-edged prosecutor, Schaeffer chose finger-pointing to dress a non-Clark-fan reader in Clark's clothes, forcing the reader to become a Marcia Clark, stationing the reader's point of view behind Clark's unlikable characteristics. The imperative voice, in tandem with the intimate and poignant details of Clark's personal and professional life, helps to create a more sympathetic portrait of Clark. On the other hand, the imperative voice gives readers already sympathetic to Clark the privilege to participate in Marcia-Clark Day, the essay for those readers serves as an homage to the prosecutor. Finger Point commands often become a list, so it may be helpful to review "Netting" in the flow section of the Style unit.

There are many other tastes of "Are You Talking To Me?" second person. Jamaica Kincaid's short story "Girl" is actually a list of commands written in the imperative or second person voice: "Wash the white clothes on Monday and put them on the stone heap; wash the color clothes on Tuesday and put them on the clothesline to dry." Kincaid overwhelms her reader with the unending commands and chores doled out by a nameless Mother Voice. The reader becomes the receiver of the commands, buckles under the weight of the finger-points, and so sympathizes with anyone receiving the orders.

Implied second person is the typical point of view used to explain a process or give instructions. Open up a build-your-own-furniture instruction manual or a recipe book and the second person point of view stares you in the face. More interesting are the demanding instructions in "Unchopping a Tree" by M.S. Merwin from *The Miner's Pale Daughter*. The instructions — about the meticulousness, riskiness, and compromising, all necessary for putting a tree back together after it has been chopped to pieces— become symbolic of what it takes, and what one gets, when repairing a very damaged personal, emotional relationship. The process starts with "you" taking the "leaves, the small twigs, and the nests that have been shaken, ripped, or broken off by the fall; these must be gathered and attached once again to their respective places." The instructions include warnings that give the process a metaphorical dimension: "much depends upon the size, age, shape, and species of the tree," "Finally the moment arrives when the last sustaining piece [of the scaffold] is removed and the tree stands again on its own . . . as though its weight for a moment stood on your heart," "How long will it stand there now? What more can you do?"

Prophets and preachers make more philosophical commands with implied second person point of view, some of the most poetic and meaningful ascribed to Jesus in Matthew, 5:1-7:28: "You cannot serve God and mammon . . . Do not throw your pearls before swine, lest they trample them under foot and turn to attack you," or "Enter by the narrow gate; for the gate is wide and the way is easy that leads to destruction, and those who enter by it are many. For the gate is narrow and the way is hard, that leads to life, and those who find it are few." Prophetic finger point is poignantly used in Suquamish Indian Chief Seattle's "Reply to Washington Territory Governor Isaac Stevens" in 1854, after the sale of two million acres to the federal government and before the great Indian relocations and massacres of the 1860's. The letter starts in first person then shifts to second person: "You wander far from the graves of your ancestors and seemingly without

UNCORKING 209

regret. Your religion was written upon tables of stone by the iron finger of your God so that you not forget" as opposed to the Native American's whose religion is found in the dreams of old men in "solemn hours."

As with Chief Seattle's letter, often finger point enters a piece unexpectedly. "The Art of Teaching Science" by Lewis Thomas for *New York Times* was written while he was chancellor of the Sloan-Kettering Cancer Center. Thomas's speech also starts in first person and then shifts to second, in order to stress what needs to be done to teach science effectively: "You cannot possibly teach quantum mechanics without mathematics, to be sure, but you can describe the strangeness of the world opened up by quantum theory . . . that there are deep mysteries and profound paradoxes . . . Do not teach that biology is a useful perhaps profitable science; that can come later. . . Teach ecology early on. Let it be understood that the earth's life is a system . . . held in an almost unbelievably improbable state of regulated balance" His lines continue to be prophetic.

Third person: Talking about a group that embodies a particular mentality or philosophical perspective in terms of one single person, in other words third person singular (he, she, or it), instead of third person plural (they), offers other possibilities for disarming. The writer assigns a long lists of particulars to one single person that in reality could only be found among several people of the target group. Germain Greer does this in her landmark book *The Female Eunuch.* She wants to shatter the stereotypic self-indulged woman. When all the items that these women desire as a group are assigned to a single, indefinite "she," for a split second the reader associates all the items listed weighted on one person, rendering this person a grotesque composite.

For Greer this creates an ugly giant, a cosmic vacuum cleaner, sucking up all that the natural world has to offer: "She is the crown of creation, the masterpiece. The depths of the sea are ransacked for pearl and coral to deck her; the bowels of the earth are laid open that she might wear gold, sapphires, diamonds, and rubies. Baby seals are battered with staves, unborn lambs ripped from their mothers' wombs, millions of moles, muskrats, squirrels, minks, ermines, foxes, beavers, chinchillas, ocelots, lynxes, and other small and lovely creatures die untimely deaths that she might have furs." Later the parts of many ad-page women merge into a giant plastic doll whose "glossy lips and mat complexion, her unfocused eyes and flawless fingers, her extraordinary hair all floating shining, curling and gleaming, reveal the inhuman triumph of cosmetics, lighting, focusing and printing, cropping and composition." Such constant Netting allows a writer to build a cartoon that uncorks anyone who identifies with any part of this exaggerated, third person composite.

Another strong taste of "Are You Talking To Me?" by building an ugly giant is "Shipping Out" by David Foster for *Harper's Magazine,* a hilarious attack on ship cruising . It never looked worse than after the lists of grotesque perspectives on recreation, food, attitude, and environment that make this lengthy article hard to put down. Smelling "suntan lotion spread over 2,100 pounds of hot flesh" is only the start of this voyage of horror.

Because it turns a group into an ugly giant, the third person usage of "Are You Talking to Me?" effectively smashes the groupthink faith held by readers who argue the validity of a position or mentality based on the fact that everyone else is doing or believing it, often referred to as the *bandwagon fallacy.* Conformity is irrelevant to the validity of a position because what others do or think can be right or wrong, strong or weak, but those realities can only be decided through the process described in the Thought unit. We all know examples in history where masses of people held horrible, regrettable political, scientific, spiritual, or aesthetic positions in order to conform. Third person "Are You Talking to Me?" uncorks conformity.

WORKOUT: To disarm, you may use second or third person. If you use second person to disarm, you are going to give metaphorical instructions like Merwin does above about unchopping a tree. English teachers call instruction essays process

UNCORKING

papers, but you will take the genre to a more interesting level. First decide on a topic. You will disarm a group or person that holds simplistic attitudes — about relationships, education, financial success, morality, business ethics, religion, raising children — by giving that group or person complex instructions on how to do something mundane and unrelated such as chopping or unchopping a tree, making or unmaking a cake, creating or dismantling a legal process. These subjects act as a scrim to camouflage your true message.

Next, find a format for the instructions: furniture instructions for putting together a cabinet, a recipe for a Thanksgiving turkey, step-by-step instructions for doing your own divorce or for using a cappuccino maker. You will borrow the format, and even some of the content, of one of these, but change the material slightly so that the instructions now hint at being about the topic which you picked above. Instructions usually use an implied second person, but rewrite them so that they use "you" directly at the beginning of many of your sentences.

The "real" instructions are usually devoid of sensual clues and metaphors. When you rewrite, add these too, just enough so that your reader can tell that the instructions you are giving hint at being a metaphor for something else. In *The Size of Thoughts*, Nicholson Baker includes a recipe for hot sauce to put on ice cream, but fills out a typical recipe with sensory details and suggestions for attitude which are normally left out of literal instructions: "Entertain yourself by breaking the ingot of chocolate into its two halves and pushing the halves and the subsiding chunk of butter around with the tip of the butter knife. Then abandon the butter knife and switch to a spoon." or "Stir idly." or "you'll be able to brandish the whole solidified disk of chocolate merely by lifting the spoon. It looks like a metal detector."

Like Baker, make your instructions more sensual and mental than typical directions, but also make them more metaphorical. For instance, in a book which shows how to prepare your own will, step four outlines instructions for community property ownership problems: "If a significant amount of your property came from a personal injury settlement and you and your spouse disagree as to how it should be left, you will want to check the specifics of your state's law." Let us pretend that you have decided to use this format and subject as a metaphor which disarms simple-minded views on how people learn. You call the essay "Transferring Your Knowledge to Your Lover." When you are at the place in your instructions where the above line could occur, you might write the following: "If a significant amount of your knowledge came from suffering and you and your parents disagree as to how to leave it with others, you will want to check with Shakespeare's *King Lear*."

If you use third person for uncorking, create an ugly giant. Pick one target group: fast food gulpers, prideful athletes, English teachers, religious leaders, computer sales people, sentimental aunts and uncles. Before you start writing, create categories: the group's most important issues, ritual objects, clothes, dialogue for specific situations, diets, ambitions, self-images, and anything else you wish to write about concerning your target group. You will need at least ten categories. Second, list five to ten individual responses under each of your categories. For instance, if you were writing about prideful athletes, one of the categories might be dialogue you have heard individuals of the group use to flirt and hustle the opposite sex. Write down five to ten of these lines. Interview members or hang out in locker rooms and eavesdrop on conversations. For other categories, visit the library.

Finally you are ready to write your paper. Use the flow techniques to sweep together all the details under each category together into sentences so that, connected under third person, you create a third person singular ugly giant. For instance, in the example above, you will have "He says," not "They say," followed by a list of flirtatious remarks that actually come from five to ten members of the group. The third person singular point of view sucks group characteristics into one swollen vat and then pops the group's plug.

SINCERELY YOURS

One of the most sincere and potent ways of disarming is writing a letter. Most English classes teach how to write business letters, turning letters into a business suit with a tie. Form letters are shred material, disappointing because letter writing comes with an expectation of being more personal: Unlike books and essays, letters are hidden in envelopes, to be opened only by the addressed individual. When not dressed up, most people think of letters as slobs at the beach: show-off post cards with simplistic having-a-great-time and five-second thoughtfulnesses scrawled on the back. The best letters, including the best business letters, will always be those that are carefully thought out and directed to a small group of people or to a particular person. These letters can carry a strong disarming potion known as intimacy.

Even when we accept that letters are supposed to be intimate, most people rely more on barfing their feelings into the envelope rather than building a careful, persuasive perspective, well supported by details. One of the most famous letters ever written was writer Franz Kafka's 1919 letter to his father. One of the beginning sentences best describes the advantages of using letters to disarm: "Dear Father: You asked me recently why I maintain that I am afraid of you. As usual, I was unable to think of any answer to your question, partly for the very reason that I am afraid of you, and partly because any explanation of the grounds for this fear would mean going into far more details than I could even approximately keep in mind while talking." The letter continues for sixty pages, outlining evidence of his father's hypocrisy, egocentricism, smugness, control strategies, arrogance, and belittlings.

One of the best developed letters we have seen was published in *Harper's Magazine* by the famous Hollywood script writer Joe Eszterhaus and written to Michael Ovitz, then the head of the most powerful Hollywood talent source, Creative Arts Agency. Ovitz had threatened Eszterhaus with having his foot soldiers "blow [his] brains out" all because Eszterhaus wanted his old friend and first agent, Guy McElwaine, to represent him, and Ovitz felt threatened because Eszterhaus brought in about $1.25 million a screenplay. The first part of the letter, without any anger in Eszterhaus's voice, carefully outline's Ovitz's threats, as well as several of Ovitz's lieutenant Rand Hoston's comments such as, "Mike's going to put you into the fucking ground."

The second part of the letter explains what Eszterhaus believes is wrong with Ovitz's comments: how it is cliché gangster movie blackmail, what the role of agents should be, how clients are not agent's possessions. The third part of the letter explains what Eszterhaus intends to do about Ovitz's threats, including discussions with his family and a decision to stay in an older house, putting an expensive home they had just purchased up for sale. At this point, the letter has been fairly long, but calm and detailed, and only at the very end of the letter does Joe Eszterhaus tell Ovitz off: "So do whatever you want to do, Mike, and fuck you. I have my family and I have my old imperfect manual typewriter, and they have always been the things I've treasured the most."

If Eszterhaus had said "fuck you" at the beginning, the letter would have been tossed, not only by Ovitz, but by everyone else, including the Writers Guild of America, who came to Eszterhaus's rescue and backed Ovitz down. By the end of the letter, which has been so well documented, the reader is beginning to whisper "fuck you" to Ovitz too, so that when Eszterhaus says it, the reader applauds. Profanity is only justified by the proper context. On the other hand, a letter from D. C. Dumbass in Westminster, California to the editor of *Thrasher*, a monthly magazine about skate boarding, starts "All right, call me a dumbfuck, but I just found out the other day that Washington, D.C., isn't in the state

UNCORKING 215

of Washington." Here the profanity comes at the beginning, but it is self-deprecating, directed only at the writer himself; so in this context the profanity seems acceptable. This letter is short and ends with an angry denunciation of everyone for never educating him, but it stays funny and sincere so we take his complaint seriously and feel society has been properly disarmed for a Geography education glitch.

Style and organization are both key to how well a letter disarms with its sincerity. Sometimes styles can be mixed in a letter. This happens in "An Open Letter to M. Jacques Chirac" by Bob Millington in *The Age,* a Melbourne, Australia newspaper. The letter, discovered by *Harper's Magazine,* is addressed to French president Chirac when he announced France would resume its nuclear testing program by staging more explosions in the South Pacific near Australia. What makes the letter especially disarming is that it mixes French and English to create a sarcastic tone that also chop-livers French language purity. The letter starts, "Je suis a bit fromaged off avec votre decision to blow up La Pacifique avec les Frog bombes nuclears," and ends with "Reconsider, mon ami. Otherwise in les hotels et estaminets de l'Australie le curse anciens d'Angleterre — 'Damnation to the French'—will be heard un autre temps. Votre chums don't want that."

WORKOUT: Write a letter to someone to whom you have something very important to say, but what you have to say involves a truth that would be so devastating to the receiver that you could not send the letter. The letter could be to anyone personally important to you: a family member, an employer or employee, a lover, a friend, someone dead or alive, a teacher or coach. To truly test your control with an emotionally charged issue, it is important that the letter is about an injustice that you witnessed first hand and that the letter would have serious fall out for you if you sent it. Once you have actually written the letter, you may decide that you really should send the letter after all, or more likely, you will decide to burn it. Letter writing does not always need to result in sending a letter. A letter writer confronts a recipient with the same emotional intensity whether the would-be recipient actually receives the letter or not; yet the writer's deep, inner feelings are released and clarified in the letter writing process whether the letter is sent or not.

Follow Eszterhaus's procedure described above: First outline the injustice in complete detail without using any judgment or anger in your tone so that the receiver cannot deny what happened. In the second part of the letter, explain what was wrong with the unjust action. Many will admit to doing what they are accused of if their actions and words are carefully documented in the first part of the letter, but still the recipient will fail to see what was wrong with what was done or will rationalize it away. Do not let the person do that. Make the injustice clear, explaining how it is both hurtful to others and the recipient's self. Wait until the end to suggest your present position and make sure any telling-off is commiserate with the crime. Always assume someone else will be reading the letter; you want them to follow your line of thinking and come to the same conclusion you have come to.

COOL DOWN: Rewrite your letter with style. Too often people think they have said enough by pouring their guts out. All writing, even letter writing, becomes more effective, more accurate, more readable, and reflects more of the writer's attitude when it has flow, pause, and fusion.

ORDER FORM

Mail Orders: Verve Press, P.O. Box 1997, Huntington Beach, CA 92647. See form below.
Retail Bookstores: Have your bookstore order from whole salers such as Baker & Taylor or Ingrams.
Textbook orders: Campus bookstores should order directly from Verve Press above with a purchase order. SAN 6590598

Please send me a copy of **Adíos, Strunk & White**, retail $12.95. If I order directly from Verve Press, Verve Press will pay my California sales tax. (Allow a few weeks delivery for book rate.)

CHECK ALL THAT APPLY (Note: all prices are subject to change):

— **I can't wait for book rate.** Please send the book Priority Mail. I've added $3.00 to the price for the first book and $2.00 for each additional book for shipping and handling.

— **Standard retail customer order.** Please find a check for the price of each book ($12.95 plus $1.50 book rate shipping)

— **Educator's discount order.** Since this book is a writer's resource book as well as a textbook, I understand there are no free examination copies of the book. Please find either a personal check or a purchase order from my campus for a 50% educator's discount per book. Send the book to my campus address listed below. ($6.47 plus $1.50 book rate shipping)

— **Complimentary copy with classroom order:** I have enclosed a photocopy of my classroom order for 10 or more copies of **Adíos, Strunk & White**, therefore please send me a complimentary copy to my campus address listed below.

— **Customized syllabus:** I teach writing and would like to pay to have Gary & Glynis Hoffman co-ordinate my essay reader with all of the sections in **Adíos, Strunk and White**. Please have them contact me at the campus address below to discuss terms. (Include the name, author, and publisher of your reader.)

School Name (if applicable): _____

Name : _____

Address: _____

City: _____

State: _____ Zip: _____

Telephone: (_____) _____

ORDER FORM

Mail Orders: Verve Press, P.O. Box 1997, Huntington Beach, CA 92647. See form below.

Retail Bookstores: Have your bookstore order from whole salers such as Baker & Taylor or Ingrams.

Textbook orders: Campus bookstores should order directly from Verve Press above with a purchase order. SAN 6590598

Please send me a copy of **Adíos, Strunk & White**, retail $12.95. If I order directly from Verve Press, Verve Press will pay my California sales tax. (Allow a few weeks delivery for book rate.)

CHECK ALL THAT APPLY (Note: all prices are subject to change):

— **I can't wait for book rate.** Please send the book Priority Mail. I've added $3.00 to the price for the first book and $2.00 for each additionalbook for shipping and handling.

— **Standard retail customer order.** Please find a check for the price of each book ($12.95 plus $1.50 book rate shipping)

— **Educator's discount order.** Since this book is a writer's resource book as well as a textbook, I understand there are no free examination copies of the book. Please find either a personal check or a purchase order from my campus for a 50% educator's discount per book. Send the book to my campus address listed below. ($6.47 plus $1.50 book rate shipping)

— **Complimentary copy with classroom order:** I have enclosed a photocopy of my classroom order for 10 or more copies of **Adíos, Strunk & White**, therefore please send me a complimentary copy to my campus address listed below.

— **Customized syllabus:** I teach writing and would like to pay to have Gary & Glynis Hoffman co-ordinate my essay reader with all of the sections in **Adíos, Strunk and White**. Please have them contact me at the campus address below to discuss terms. (Include the name, author, and publisher of your reader.)

School Name (if applicable): _____

Name : _____

Address: _____

City: _____

State: _____ Zip: _____

Telephone: (_____) _____

ORDER FORM

Mail Orders: Verve Press, P.O. Box 1997, Huntington Beach, CA 92647. See form below.

Retail Bookstores: Have your bookstore order from whole salers such as Baker & Taylor or Ingrams.

Textbook orders: Campus bookstores should order directly from Verve Press above with a purchase order. SAN 6590598

Please send me a copy of **Adíos, Strunk & White, retail $12.95.** If I order directly from Verve Press, Verve Press will pay my California sales tax. (Allow a few weeks delivery for book rate.)

CHECK ALL THAT APPLY (Note: all prices are subject to change):

— **I can't wait for book rate.** Please send the book Priority Mail. I've added $3.00 to the price for the first book and $2.00 for each additional book for shipping and handling.

— **Standard retail customer order.** Please find a check for the price of each book ($12.95 plus $1.50 book rate shipping)

— **Educator's discount order.** Since this book is a writer's resource book as well as a textbook, I understand there are no free examination copies of the book. Please find either a personal check or a purchase order from my campus for a 50% educator's discount per book. Send the book to my campus address listed below. ($6.47 plus $1.50 book rate shipping)

— **Complimentary copy with classroom order:** I have enclosed a photocopy of my classroom order for 10 or more copies of **Adíos, Strunk & White,** therefore please send me a complimentary copy to my campus address listed below.

— **Customized syllabus**: I teach writing and would like to pay to have Gary & Glynis Hoffman co-ordinate my essay reader with all of the sections in **Adíos, Strunk and White.** Please have them contact me at the campus address below to discuss terms. (Include the name, author, and publisher of your reader.)

School Name (if applicable): _____

Name : _____

Address: _____

City: _____

State: _____ Zip: _____

Telephone: (_____) _____